BILLY BUDD, SAILOR

Herman Melville

EDITORIAL DIRECTOR Justin Kestler
MANAGING EDITOR Ben Florman

SERIES EDITORS Boomie Aglietti, Justin Kestler
PRODUCTION Christian Lorentzen

WRITERS Jim Cocola, Brian Phillips
EDITORS John Crowther, Jesse Hawkes

This edition published by Spark Publishing

Spark Publishing
A Division of SparkNotes LLC
120 Fifth Avenue, 8th Floor
New York, NY 10011

02 03 04 05 SN 9 8 7 6 5 4 3 2 1

Please send all comments and questions or report errors to
feedback@sparknotes.com.

Library of Congress information available upon request

Printed and bound in the United States

RRD-C

ISBN 1-58663-437-2

INTRODUCTION: STOPPING TO BUY SPARKNOTES ON A SNOWY EVENING

Whose words these are you *think* you know.
Your paper's due tomorrow, though;
We're glad to see you stopping here
To get some help before you go.

Lost your course? You'll find it here.
Face tests and essays without fear.
Between the words, good grades at stake:
Get great results throughout the year.

Once school bells caused your heart to quake
As teachers circled each mistake.
Use SparkNotes and no longer weep,
Ace every single test you take.

Yes, books are lovely, dark, and deep,
But only what you grasp you keep,
With hours to go before you sleep,
With hours to go before you sleep.

CONTENTS

NOTE: This SparkNote is based on the reading text of *Billy Budd, Sailor* prepared by Harrison Hayford and Merton M. Sealts, Jr. This version of the text appears in the Library of America edition of Billy Budd, as well as the Penguin Classics and University of Chicago Press editions. Other editions vary in certain respects—see A NOTE ON THE TEXT, p. 3, for a fuller explanation.

CONTEXT

ERMAN MELVILLE WAS BORN in New York City in 1819, the third of eight children born to Maria Gansevoort Melville and Allan Melville, a prosperous importer of foreign goods. When the family business failed at the end of the 1820s, the Melvilles relocated to Albany in an attempt to revive their fortune. In another string of bad luck, overwork drove Allan to an early grave, and the young Herman was forced to start working in a bank at the age of thirteen.

After a few more years of formal education, Melville left school at eighteen to become an elementary school teacher. This career was abruptly cut short and followed by a brief tenure as a newspaper reporter. Running out of alternatives on land, Melville made his first sea voyage at nineteen, as a merchant sailor on a ship bound for Liverpool, England. He returned to America the next summer, to seek his fortune in the West. After briefly settling in Illinois, he went back east in the face of continuing financial difficulties.

Finally, driven to desperation at twenty-one, Melville committed to a whaling voyage, of indefinite destination and scale, on board a ship called the *Acushnet*. This journey took him around the continent of South America, across the Pacific Ocean, and to the South Seas, where he abandoned ship with a fellow sailor in the summer of 1842, eighteen months after setting out from New York. The two men found themselves in the Marquesas Islands, where they accidentally wandered into the company of a tribe of cannibals. Lamed by an injury to his leg, Melville became separated from his companion and spent a month alone in the company of the natives. This experience later formed the core of his first novel, *Typee: A Peep at Polynesian Life,* published in 1846. An indeterminate mixture of fact and fiction, Melville's fanciful travel narrative remained the most popular and successful of his works during his lifetime.

Life among these natives and numerous other exotic experiences abroad provided Melville with endless literary conceits. Armed with the voluminous knowledge obtained from constant reading while at sea, Melville set out to write a series of novels detailing his adventures and his philosophy of life. *Typee* was followed by *Omoo* (1847) and *Mardi and a Voyage Thither* (1849), two more novels about his Polynesian experiences. *Redburn*, also published in 1849, is a fictionalized account of Melville's first voyage to Liverpool. His next novel, *White-Jacket; or The World in a Man-of-War*, published in 1850, is a more generalized and allegorical account of life at sea aboard a warship.

Through the lens of literary history, these first five novels are all seen as a prologue to the work that is today considered Melville's masterpiece, *Moby-Dick; or The Whale*, which first appeared in 1851. A story of monomania aboard a whaling ship, *Moby-Dick* is a tremendously ambitious novel that functions at once as a documentary of life at sea and a vast philosophical allegory of life in general. No sacred subject is spared in this bleak and scathing critique of the known world, as Melville satirizes by turns religious traditions, moral values, and the literary and political figures of the day.

Motivated to the passionate intensity of *Moby-Dick* in part by a burgeoning friendship with Nathaniel Hawthorne, Melville was unperturbed by the lukewarm reception that his grandest novel enjoyed in the initial reviews. However, Melville reevaluated his place in the literary world after the outraged reaction to his next novel, *Pierre; or The Ambiguities*, which appeared in 1852. The sole pastoral romance among Melville's works, this self-described "rural bowl of milk" became known as a decidedly bad book as much for its sloppy writing as for its incestuous theme and nebulous morals.

After the disastrous reception of *Pierre*, Melville turned his attentions to the short story. In the following five years, he published numerous fictional sketches of various lengths in several prominent periodicals of the day. Most notable among these works are "Bartelby, The Scrivener" and "Benito Cereno." In this period, he also published his final two completed novels: a historical work titled *Israel Potter; or Fifty Years of Exile*, in 1855, and a maddeningly bleak satire of trust titled *The Confidence Man: His Masquerade*, in 1857.

In the remaining thirty-five years of his life, Melville's literary production cooled considerably, grinding nearly to a halt. A brief stint on the national lecture tour gave way to more stable employment as a customshouse inspector, a job he held for almost twenty years before his retirement in the late 1880s. A volume of war poetry, *Battle-Pieces and Aspects of the War*, appeared in 1866, and Melville published the lengthy poem *Clarel: A Poem and Pilgrimage in the Holy Land* in 1876. Toward the end of his life,

Melville produced two more volumes of verse, *John Marr and Other Sailors* (1888) and *Timoleon* (1891).

At the time of his death in 1891, Melville had recently completed his first extended prose narrative in more than thirty years. However, this work would remain unpublished for yet another thirty years, appearing in 1924 in a limited London edition under the title of *Billy Budd*. Only after Melville began to gain wider acclaim in the mid-twentieth century did scholars and general readers begin to read *Billy Budd* with serious care. Based in part on events Melville himself experienced at sea, *Billy Budd* also incorporates a historical incident involving Melville's first cousin, who played a role, similar to Captain Vere, as an arbitrator in a controversy involving the trial and execution of two midshipmen on board the U.S.S. *Somers* in 1842.

Melville's first great literary historical proponent, Lewis Mumford, saw *Billy Budd* as a testament to Melville's ultimate reconciliation with the incongruities and injustices of life. According to Mumford, *Billy Budd* is the placid, accepting last word of an aged man and an affirmation of true religious transcendence. Later critics, such as Lawrance Thompson, saw in *Billy Budd* a bitter satire that served only to reconfirm Melville's earlier acerbity. According to Thompson, Melville's cynicism and defiance appear all the more heightened and corrosive for their more subtle means.

The last, long-delayed work of a long-silent author, *Billy Budd* is a unique document in American letters. It stands as one of the most ambiguous and inscrutable works of one of America's most ambiguous and inscrutable authors. The two major critical views—*Billy Budd* as religious paean, or *Billy Budd* as jaded satire—have only served to fuel the legend of *Billy Budd*. Standing in such sharp opposition to each other, these two views persist with equal vigor to the present, providing continuous debate for readers the world over.

A NOTE ON THE TEXT

Melville worked on *Billy Budd* during the final years of his life, and though he seems to have essentially finished a draft of the novel, he never prepared it for publication. When he died in 1891, he left it in the form of an extremely rough manuscript with innumerable notes and marks for correction and revision, some in his own handwriting, some in the handwriting of his wife. Undiscovered until more than thirty years after Melville's death, the novel went unpublished until 1924. Because of the indefinite state of the manuscript and the lapsed time between Melville's death and its discovery, there has been a long-standing editorial controversy with regard to how the book should be edited and arranged. As a result, there are many widely varying editions of *Billy Budd*.

Editors working directly from Melville's manuscript have produced three separate editions of the novel: one prepared by Raymond Weaver in 1924, one by F. Barron Freeman in 1948, and *two* by Harrison Hayford and Merton M. Sealts, Jr.—a reading text and a "genetic text"—in 1962. The Freeman edition is partly based on the Weaver edition, and, to make matters more complicated, the Freeman edition was reedited in 1956 by Elizabeth Treeman, who claimed to have found more than 500 errors in Freeman's work. Editors have disagreed about issues such as how authoritative the revisions in Melville's wife's handwriting really are—Weaver, in fact, mistook Elizabeth Melville's handwriting for her husband's, a mistake that earned him the scorn of subsequent editors. Other disagreements concern chapter order, the inclusion or exclusion of certain chapters Melville may have wished to cut, and the name of Billy's ship, which Melville's manuscript calls "the *Indomitable*" twenty-five times and "the *Bellipotent*" six times. Most editors have gone with "*Indomitable*," but Hayford and Sealts conclude that Melville intended to change the name to "*Bellipotent*."

Today, the Hayford/Sealts reading text is generally regarded as the best version of *Billy Budd*, though as perhaps befits a novel of such deep thematic ambiguity, a truly definitive text is impossible. Most commercially available editions are based on the Hayford/Sealts reading text, including this SparkNote, which utilizes the Library of America edition of the novel. Other editions are likely to differ widely, in the several respects mentioned above.

PLOT OVERVIEW

THE SETTING IS THE LAST DECADE of the eighteenth century. The British naval warship H.M.S. *Bellipotent* impresses, or involuntarily recruits, the young sailor Billy Budd, extracting him from duty aboard the *Rights-of-Man*, a merchant ship. Billy's commanding officer, Captain Graveling, though reluctant to let one of his best men go, has little choice in the face of the superior ship's demands. Billy packs up his gear without so much as a protest and follows the boarding officer of the *Bellipotent*, Lieutenant Ratcliffe, across the gangway to his new assignment. After a cheery good-bye to his old mates, Billy settles in quickly among the company of the *Bellipotent*. He proves most industrious and eager in his role as foretopman and soon earns the affection of his more experienced fellow sailors.

Billy is deeply affected by the sight of a violent lashing given to one of the ship's crew. Hoping to avoid a similar punishment, Billy attempts to fulfill his duties in model fashion, but finds himself under constant scrutiny due to various minor infractions. Puzzled by this persecution, Billy seeks out the advice of the Dansker, an aged, experienced sailor. After explaining the situation to him, the Dansker concludes that Claggart, the master-at-arms, holds a grudge against Billy. Refusing to accept this theory, Billy dismisses the Dansker's opinion but continues to wonder pensively about his situation.

Shortly thereafter, at a lunchtime meal, Billy accidentally spills his soup pan in the ship's dining room after a sudden lurch. The contents of the pan trickle to the feet of the passing Claggart, who makes an offhand, seemingly lighthearted remark in recognition of the spill. His comment elicits a stream of obligatory laughter from the ship's company, and Billy interprets the event as proof of Claggart's approval. But Claggart is offended by the accident, and finds it indicative of Billy's contempt for him. He fixates on the accident as proof of Billy's hostility, and his assistant Squeak resolves to increase his surreptitious persecutions of Billy in recompense.

One night, an anonymous figure rouses Billy from his sleep on the upper deck and asks him to meet in a remote quarter of the ship. Confused, Billy mechanically obeys. At the mysterious rendezvous, Billy is puzzled when, after some vague discourse, the unidentified man flashes two guineas in exchange for a promise of cooperation.

Without comprehending the exact details of this solicitation, Billy recognizes that something is amiss, and he raises his stuttering voice and threatens the man with uncharacteristic violence. The conspirator quickly slinks into the darkness, and Billy finds himself confronted with the curious inquiries of two fellow sailors. Unsure of how to explain the situation, Billy explains that he simply happened upon a fellow sailor who was in the wrong part of the ship, and chased the man back to his proper station with a gruff rebuke.

Somewhat later, after a brief skirmish with an enemy frigate, Claggart approaches Captain Vere with news of a rumored mutiny and names Billy Budd as the ringleader of the rebellion. Vere summons Billy to his cabin and instructs Claggart to repeat his accusation. Upon hearing of this unexpected blot on his character, Billy is rendered speechless. Vere commands Billy to defend himself, but then, noticing Billy's tendency to stutter, softens his approach. Left with no other means of defense, and twisted into a rage at Claggart's outrageous words against him, Billy strikes out in a fury, giving Claggart a swift punch to the forehead.

The blow proves forceful enough to knock Claggart unconscious, and he lies bleeding from the nose and ears as Billy and Vere attempt to revive him. Abandoning this effort, Vere dismisses Billy to a neighboring stateroom until further notice. The ship's surgeon pronounces Claggart dead after a brief examination, and Captain Vere summons a group of his senior officers to the cabin.

In a decisive move, Vere calls a drumhead court consisting of the captain of the marines, the first lieutenant, and the sailing master. Vere, functioning as the main witness, gives a testimony of the relevant events to the jury. Billy remains rather silent during his period of questioning, admitting to the blow but maintaining his innocence of intention and declaring his lack of affiliation with any potential mutiny. The court dismisses Billy again to the stateroom.

During a tense period of deliberation, Vere hovers over the jury. When they seem to be deadlocked, unable to make a decision, Vere steps forward to declare his conviction that the rule of law must supersede the reservations of conscience. He concludes his speech to the jury by insisting that they decide to acquit or condemn in strict accordance with the letter of military law. After a period of further deliberation, the jury finds Billy Budd guilty as charged and sentences him to death by hanging on the following morning.

Captain Vere communicates to Billy the news of his fate and, after a discussion with him that we do not learn about directly, he withdraws to leave the prisoner by himself. Later that evening, Vere calls a general meeting of the ship's crew and explains the events of the day. Claggart receives an official burial at sea, and all hands prepare to bear witness to Billy's hanging at dawn.

Billy spends his final hours in chains on board an upper gun deck, guarded by a sentry. The ship's chaplain attempts to spiritually prepare Billy for his death, but Billy already seems to be in a state of perfect peace and resignation. As the chaplain withdraws from Billy's company, he kisses him gently on the cheek as a token of good will.

That morning, shortly after four A.M., Billy is hanged in the mainyard of the ship. As the crew watches him being strung up, preparing to die, they hear him utter his last words: "God bless Captain Vere!" The assembled company automatically echoes this unexpected sentiment, and Billy expires with surprising calm as dawn breaks over the horizon.

After Billy's death, the crew begins to murmur, but the officers quickly disperse them to various tasks. Whistles blow and the ship returns to regular business. In the ensuing days, sailors engage in various discussions concerning Billy's fate and the mysterious circumstances of his expiration. On its return voyage, the *Bellipotent* falls in with a French warship, the *Athée*, or *Atheist*. Captain Vere, wounded in the skirmish, eventually dies in a Gibraltar hospital, uttering as his last words, "Billy Budd, Billy Budd."

Finally, the legend of Billy Budd becomes recorded and institutionalized in naval circles. A newspaper reports the incident from afar, implicating Billy Budd as the villainous assailant of an innocent Claggart. The sailors themselves, however, begin to revere Billy's growing legend, treating the spar from his gallows as a holy object, and composing laudatory verse in his memory.

CHARACTER LIST

Billy Budd Discovered on a doorstep as an infant, Billy Budd is a fine physical specimen at age twenty-one, renowned for his good looks and gentle, innocent ways. Upon taking up as a young seaman in the service of His Majesty the King of England, Billy grows into the near-perfect image of what Melville calls the "Handsome Sailor," an ideal specimen who inspires love and admiration in all his fellows. While working on board the merchant ship *Rights-of-Man,* Billy is impressed into naval duty as a foretopman (a sailor who sits atop the foremast or above) on board the warship H.M.S. *Bellipotent.* Although much younger than most of the *Bellipotent*'s crewmen, the cheerful, innocent young man quickly gains back the popularity he had previously enjoyed, earning the nickname "Baby Budd" in the process. He has several shortcomings, however, including an inability to perceive ill will in other people. He also has an unpredictable tendency to stutter, and at certain crucial moments he is rendered completely speechless.

Captain the Honorable Edward Fairfax Vere Captain of the H.M.S. *Bellipotent.* A bachelor of aristocratic lineage, the forty-year-old Vere has made his mark as a distinguished sailor. His nickname, "Starry Vere," seems fitting for this abstracted, intellectual figure who often shuts himself up at sea with his books. Vere remains somewhat aloof and diffident among his peers, though he is not haughty.

John Claggart The master-at-arms of the *Bellipotent,* an office equivalent to chief of police on board the ship. Behind his back, the crew refers to Claggart with the derogatory nickname "Jemmy Legs." At age thirty-five, Claggart is lean and tall, with a protruding chin and an authoritative gaze. His brow bespeaks cleverness, and his black hair contrasts starkly with his pallid complexion. Because of his pale face, he stays out of the sun as much as possible. The narrator gives few details about Claggart's past, although speculation runs rampant among the crewmembers. It is known that after entering the navy unusually late in life, Claggart rose through the ranks to attain his present position on the strength of his sobriety, deference to authority, and patriotism. However, his compliant exterior disguises a cruel and sinister streak, which the narrator explains is actually a natural tendency toward evil and depravity.

The Dansker Billy's acquaintance and confidante aboard the *Bellipotent.* A wizened old sailor with beady eyes, the Dansker listens and occasionally issues inscrutable, oracular responses when Billy seeks out his confidence. At other times, however, the Dansker is decidedly reticent and unhelpful.

Ship's Surgeon Pronounces Claggart dead upon arriving in the captain's cabin. The surgeon considers Vere's decision to call a drumhead court somewhat abrupt and hasty. Though unable to account for Billy's unusually peaceful death in the gallows, he refuses to believe that the event is attended by supernatural circumstances.

Ship's Purser Ruddy and rotund, the purser speculates that Billy's unusually peaceful death in the gallows shows a phenomenal degree of will on Billy's behalf, perhaps revealing a superhuman power.

Ship's Chaplain Reluctantly and unsuccessfully attempts to console Billy with words from the Bible on the eve of Billy's execution. When the chaplain realizes that Billy is already peacefully resigned to his death, and that his spiritual direction cannot do anything more for Billy, he leaves, kissing Billy gently on the cheek as he goes.

Squeak Claggart's most cunning corporal. Squeak supports and fuels Claggart's contempt for Billy, and tries by various maneuvers to make Billy's life miserable.

Albert   Captain Vere's hammock boy. Trusted by the captain, Albert is sent to summon Billy to the cabin on the day Claggart accuses him.

Lieutenant Ratcliffe The brusque boarding officer of the *Bellipotent*. Lieutenant Ratcliffe selects only Billy from the company of the *Rights-of-Man* for impressment, or involuntary recruitment into naval service.

Captain Graveling Captain of the *Rights-of-Man*. At fifty, the slightly overweight Captain Graveling is a benign, conscientious shipmaster who is sorry to lose Billy Budd to the *Bellipotent*.

The Red Whiskers Billy's adversary aboard the *Rights-of-Man*. When Billy strikes him, his hatred of Billy turns to love, which both parallels and contrasts with Billy's disastrous striking of Claggart.

Red Pepper The forecastleman who reproves Billy for not taking greater disciplinary action against the stranger who tries to corrupt him.

ANALYSIS OF MAJOR CHARACTERS

BILLY BUDD

Distinguished by his striking good looks and affable nature, Billy's primary quality is his extraordinary, even disturbing innocence. At twenty-one years of age, he has never directly confronted evil. Due to his good looks, he has always been well liked and admired wherever he goes. As a result, he naïvely takes the view that other people always mean him the best. He has not developed the prudent cynicism of a figure like the Dansker, who is well aware of man's evil inclinations. He has no defense against a hateful man such as Claggart, and cannot even perceive the malice in Claggart's sarcastic comment about Billy's accident with the soup. If Billy had believed it when the Dansker told him that Claggart was plotting against Billy, he might have been able to protect himself. But Billy is blinded by his own openhearted nature, and he misjudges the malevolent Claggart as a friend.

Billy's demise is brought about by a combination of his own weaknesses and evil influences that are outside of him and beyond his comprehension. Along with his naïve trust in others, his weaknesses include his speech impediment, which renders him unable to defend himself when Claggart accuses him of mutiny. Melville presents this speech impediment as more than a physical condition, however—Billy's hesitancy and speechlessness seem directly related to his ignorance and innocence. He has no words with which to confront Claggart because he cannot understand Claggart's evil or formulate any clear thoughts about him. Faced with Claggart's lie, he can think of no way to rebut him other than with brute force. Similarly, Billy is unable to identify and condemn the conspirators on the ship adequately so as to nip the situation before it buds. Essentially, Billy's mental and emotional shortcomings render him extremely vulnerable to the evil influences on board the ship, although the evil itself lies in other people.

Melville portrays Billy's innocence as something to be both admired and pitied. In a number of ways, Billy's fate parallels that of Jesus Christ, suggesting that the sacrifice of Billy's innocence represents both a significant loss for the world and a hope for mankind's redemption. It would be a mistake, however, to view Billy simply as a Christ figure. Billy is a flawed human being, even violent at times. Unlike Christ, Billy does not willingly or even wittingly sacrifice himself for the sake of others. Whereas Christ, in his death, intentionally takes all of the sins of the world upon himself to save humankind from evil, Billy dies because he cannot comprehend evil or defend himself adequately against it. In this sense, Billy is more human than Christ—what happens to Billy more closely resembles something that could happen to us, and we are perhaps able to pity him and empathize with him more deeply.

CHARACTER ANALYSIS

CLAGGART

> *With no power to annul the elemental evil in him, though readily enough he could hide it; apprehending the good, but powerless to be it; a nature like Claggart's, surcharged with energy as such natures almost invariably are, what recourse is left to it but to recoil upon itself and, like the scorpion for which the Creator alone is responsible, act out to the end the part allotted it.* (See QUOTATIONS, p. 57)

If Billy represents innocence in the novel, the older, higher-ranked Claggart represents evil. Claggart's innate wickedness is causeless and seemingly limitless. His motives are far more sophisticated and subtle than Billy can comprehend. Billy lacks awareness of the discrepancies that exist between human action and human intention, always taking actions at face value; Claggart, on the other hand, exhibits a great understanding of deception and ambiguity and makes frequent use of them in his nefarious plots—for instance, he shows kindness toward Billy to mask his unkind intentions.

Because Claggart carefully hides his own motives and intentions, he has a tendency to assume that other people are also motivated by hidden malice, and he overinterprets the actions of others in order to find the ill will concealed within them. Deeply egocentric, Claggart obtains sustenance from envy. When Billy spills the soup, Claggart assumes that Billy has purposely directed this action toward him, utterly ignoring the obvious indication that Billy simply spilled by accident. Seeking to destroy Billy, Claggart employs underhanded and vicious methods, falsely accusing Billy of mutiny in order to see him killed.

In the novel's Christian allegory, Claggart represents Satan, working tirelessly to pervert goodness and defeat morality and human trust. On another level, Claggart represents the serpent that tempted Adam and Eve in the Garden of Eden. When Claggart's false allegation prompts Billy to strike him violently, Claggart has effectively coaxed Billy into abandoning his virtue and committing an evil deed. Indeed, the narrator refers to Claggart's corpse as a dead snake. Thus, it is possible to interpret Billy's death as a double victory for Claggart: Billy dies, as Claggart wished, and he falls from moral grace, as well.

CAPTAIN VERE

Vere symbolizes the conflict between the individual's inner self and the role society forces the individual to play. Vere likes Billy and distrusts Claggart, and he seems not to believe Claggart's accusations against Billy. When Billy strikes Claggart, Vere feels sympathy toward Billy; he does not seem to believe that Billy has committed a terrible sin. However, Vere ignores his inner emotions, convenes a court to try Billy, and urges the jury to disregard their own feelings of compassion and punish Billy according to the letter of the law.

As a man, Vere exonerates Billy, but as a ship's captain, he finds himself duty-bound to punish him, allowing his role as a captain to supersede his inner conscience. He does this partly to avoid taking responsibility for Billy's death, making him the parallel of Pontius Pilate in the novel's Christian allegory. But he also sacrifices Billy because he believes in the ultimate supremacy of society's laws over the desires and impulses of individuals. With this belief, and in his actions throughout the later part of the novel, Vere demonstrates that he places greater faith in reason and rational philosophy than he does in the dictates of his own heart. Famous for his wide reading and his love of philosophy, Vere is in some ways too cerebral to be a leader of men, and in his rigorous adherence to the rule of law he fails in his moral responsibility to Billy.

We are likely to feel that Vere is wrong in applying the letter of the law rather than following his heart, and one of the basic questions that this novel poses is why Vere is wrong to do this. One possible explanation may be that the rules governing the treatment of someone in Billy's situation are predicated on mistrust and cynicism about human beings. In the eyes of the law, someone who strikes and kills his accuser, as Billy does, *must* be guilty of murder, and is probably guilty of the crime for which he was initially accused, as well. Billy's individual circumstances are too unique and complex to be taken into consideration within the law. The novel remains ambiguous about which is paramount, the good of society or the good of the individual; still, it does make clear that Vere is racked with guilt after putting the law ahead of his conscience. Vere's last words before he dies are a repetition of Billy's name, suggesting that he is unable to let go of his sense of debt to Billy.

THEMES, MOTIFS & SYMBOLS

THEMES

Themes are the fundamental and often universal ideas explored in a literary work.

THE INDIVIDUAL VERSUS SOCIETY

Melville is deeply interested in the ways in which society forces people to curtail or limit their individuality. When the warship *Bellipotent* extracts the unassuming Billy from his former ship, the *Rights-of-Man*, the symbolism is relatively explicit: society is all-powerful, it compels men into participation in war, and in doing so it can readily dispense with the rights of the individual. The names of the ships alone—Bellipotent means "power of war"—suggest as much.

Captain Vere's dilemma in dealing with Billy illustrates how society requires the separation of one's inner feelings from one's social obligations. In prosecuting Billy, Vere decides to follow the letter of the law, despite his own sense that Billy personifies goodness and innocence. Feeling the pressure of his position as a leader with a responsibility to see that the men obey the Mutiny Act, Vere forces himself to disregard his own feelings about Billy's situation and even urges the jurors in the case to do the same. Laws, not the dictates of individual conscience, govern society; in order to fill a social role well, it may sometimes be necessary to act against one's own impulses. To be a "good" captain, Vere must do something that he instinctually interprets as morally wrong—condemning an innocent soul. Being a good captain requires him to be a bad friend to Billy, just as being a good friend to Billy would require him to be a bad captain.

In presenting Vere's dilemma, the narrator introduces a lengthy discussion about the famous mutiny at Nore. The narrator shows that most of the participants in the mutiny ultimately redeem themselves in the momentous victory at Trafalgar, where they display true patriotism. The narrator's point seems to be that the impulses of individuals are generally good and beneficial to society as a whole. However, the outcome of the narrator's story is more ominous. Although the British war machine greatly benefits from the individual enthusiasm and patriotism of its sailors, the more powerful the navy becomes, the more it is able to squelch individualism. In fact, the harsh legislation of the Mutiny Act is passed to suppress any further murmurings of dissent. Melville seems to suggest that ultimately, the individual's attempt to assert himself in the face of society will prove futile.

CONSCIENCE VERSUS LAW

Although a number of the characters in *Billy Budd* possess strong individual consciences; fundamentally, the people on the ship are unable to trust one another. Paranoia abounds. Consequently, life aboard the ship is governed by a strict set of rules, and everybody trusts the rules—not the honor or conscience of individuals—to maintain order. The mistrust that the characters feel, and that is likely also to affect us as we read, stems from the sense that evil is pervasive. Evil men like Claggart seem to be lurking everywhere. Because it is impossible to know for sure whether people's intentions are good or evil, the evil men not only disguise their own insidious designs, they also impute evil motives to others. Most notably, Claggart misinterprets Billy's intention in the soup-spilling incident and subsequently plots his downfall.

The Dansker understands this sort of dishonesty all too well, and as a result, he has acquired a cynicism in his dealings with other people. The Dansker's reticence may be interpreted in different ways, but one plausible interpretation is that he fails to take direct action against evil men because he fears the consequences of confronting evil directly, thus leaving other good men like Billy to fend for themselves. He may represent people who play roles in order to fit into society, never fully acting on their own impulses and distancing themselves from the rest of society. In this reading, the Dansker confronts a dilemma similar to Vere's. The Dansker likes Billy and tries to help him, but he ultimately sacrifices Billy to the claustrophobic, paranoid world of the ship, in which men are disconnected from their own consciences. In *Billy Budd,* men who confront the law and men who confront evil suffer similar consequences, suggesting the dark view that evil and the law are closely connected.

THE VULNERABILITY OF INNOCENCE

Billy Budd does not represent goodness so much as he does innocence, and the conflict between *innocence* and evil in this novel is different from the conflict between *good* and evil. The narrator makes clear that Billy is not a hero in the traditional sense. Though he has the good looks and blithe attitude of the ideal Handsome Sailor, his defining characteristic is extreme naïveté, not moral strength or courage. Billy does not have a sufficient awareness of good and evil to choose goodness consciously, let alone champion it. Because he is unable to recognize evil when confronted by it, he ultimately allows Claggart to draw him away from virtue and into violence.

As a youthful, handsome, and popular sailor, Billy wishes only to be well liked and well-adjusted in his social role. He assumes that no one has cause to dislike him, and takes everyone at face value. Claggart, on the other hand, is full of deception, distrust, and malice, and interprets Billy's placidity as a dangerous façade. Claggart seems to destroy Billy for no reason other than the latter's innocence. Evil exists to corrupt innocence, and even though Billy kills Claggart, in a sense Claggart achieves a double victory over Billy in his own death. Claggart's actions cause Billy to fall from both social and moral grace by committing murder, and Billy suffers death as a consequence.

MOTIFS

Motifs are recurring structures, contrasts, or literary devices that can help to develop and inform the text's major themes.

CHRISTIAN ALLEGORY

Although the narrator rarely alludes to the Bible explicitly, *Billy Budd* contains many implicit allusions to the imagery, language, and stories of the Bible, creating a sustained parallel between Billy's story and Christ's Passion, the story of Christ's suffering and death on the cross. Like Christ, Billy sacrifices his life as the innocent victim of a hostile society. Vere's role in the story parallels that of Pontius Pilate in the Gospels, as he is the official who permits the sacrifice by following the letter of the law instead of his own conscience. Claggart functions as a satanic figure, tempting Billy into evil and working to destroy him throughout the novel. Satan is not a part of the story of Christ's Passion, and Claggart's temptation of Billy more closely mirrors the serpent's temptation of Adam and Eve in the Garden of Eden than anything in the Gospels. The narrator makes Claggart's connection to the serpent in Genesis more explicit by comparing Claggart's dead body to the corpse of a snake. In addition to these main parallels, the novel's innumerable Christian references form a complex web of associations and contrasts. Critics remain sharply divided over whether *Billy Budd*'s religious imagery represents Melville's embrace of religion or harsh critique of it, which illustrates the ambiguity of the religious allegory in the story. Melville leaves to each reader the decision of what the connection between Billy Budd and Christianity signifies.

Suggestive Names

Throughout the novel, Melville uses names to indicate ideas about the true nature of people and things. For example, Billy's last name, Budd, suggests his innocence and youth by conjuring an image of a flower's bud. Captain Vere's name suggests his tendency to veer between attitudes. The name of the *Rights-of-Man* suggests the greater individual liberties enjoyed by the crew of that happier ship, while the name of the *Bellipotent* suggests its association with war and the power represented by its military order. The name of the *Athée* means "the atheist," and when this ship defeats the *Bellipotent*—which carries the characters who stand for Christian figures—the event suggests that Christian society moves toward a disastrous fall from grace as it becomes more dependent on violence and military discipline.

Primitive and Animal Imagery

The narrator frequently uses animal imagery to describe both Billy and his fellow sailors. For example, the narrator remarks that Billy appears to have the "self-consciousness" of a Saint Bernard. Later, the narrator says that Billy "was like a young horse fresh from the pasture suddenly inhaling a vile whiff from some chemical factory" when presented with the conspiratorial bribe. Again, during the trial, Billy gives Vere a questioning look "not unlike that which a dog of generous breed might turn upon his master." When he lashes out at Claggart, Billy is said to resemble a cornered dog or caged monkey. This animal imagery functions primarily to highlight Billy's extreme innocence, suggesting moreover that he is distanced from society because he lacks the proper vocabulary to understand social interactions. Melville combines this animal imagery with references to Billy as a "babe," a "savage," and an "upright barbarian," suggesting that Billy represents Melville's exploration of what happens to the natural or primitive man when confronted with the law and Christianity.

MUTINY

Mutiny figures prominently in the plot and historical background of *Billy Budd,* and it relates to numerous themes as well. The feigned mutinous conspiracy presented to Billy by the anonymous stranger on the upper deck ultimately leads to his demise. The narrator spends much time detailing the mutinies that ultimately led to the Mutiny Act, the law that necessitates Vere's condemnation of Billy. On the one hand, mutiny represents opposition to war. It also represents individuality and agency in the face of authority. Still, since a successful mutiny requires the cooperation of many sailors, it also represents a form of society. Moreover, this association defines itself in opposition to an authoritarian force that aims to keep men separated from their fellow dissenters. Thus, the captains whistle the men back to their individual duties quickly whenever they hear a murmur in the crowd.

SYMBOLS

Symbols are objects, characters, figures, or colors used to represent abstract ideas or concepts.

THE SHIPS

Broadly speaking, the H.M.S. *Bellipotent* symbolizes society, with the actions of a few characters standing for the state of human society in general. In a sense, the various ships in the novel represent different types of societies: the *Rights-of-Man* symbolizes a place where individuals maintain their individuality, while the *Bellipotent* represents a military world in which, under the threat of violence—and therefore in the presence of evil—the rules of society impinge upon the individual rights of men. The *Athée,* whose name means "the atheist" in French, symbolizes the anti-religious aspects of a powerful, war-driven society.

THE PURSER AND THE SURGEON

The purser and the surgeon who debate Billy's story after his death represent faith and skepticism, the two fundamentally opposed attitudes toward religious mysteries. The purser believes that Billy's death indicates some special quality in Billy, possibly supernatural.

The surgeon, on the other hand, maintaining a scientific viewpoint, refuses to acknowledge Billy's unusually peaceful death as more than a quirk of matter. Besides dramatizing two long-standing attitudes toward religion, these two characters and their conversation are important because they initiate the narrator's exploration of Billy's posthumous legend. The narrator ultimately calls into question the novel's larger Christian allegory as he investigates how people transform events into legendary narratives.

Summary & Analysis

Chapters 1–2

Summary: Chapter 1

The narrator begins the story by recalling a time, in the days before steamships, when it was common to observe in port towns a group of sailors gathered around a "Handsome Sailor" type—a man who stood out from his peers by being taller, stronger, and more physically attractive. The Handsome Sailor's peers would instinctively look up to and follow this naturally superior specimen. As an example, the narrator cites an instance in Liverpool in which he observed a male African in a plaid cap promenading proudly in the company of his fellow seamen.

At twenty-one years old, though young-looking for his age, Billy Budd exemplifies the Handsome Sailor type. He has only recently entered into the service of the British naval forces. In the summer of 1797, while returning to the British Isles on board the merchant ship *Rights-of-Man*, he is impressed into duty by the H.M.S. *Bellipotent*, a warship in need of extra sailors.

Billy is the only member of his company on the *Rights-of-Man* selected to change ranks by the representative of the *Bellipotent*, Lieutenant Ratcliffe. Without complaint, Billy accepts his reassignment, much to Ratcliffe's satisfaction. However, this shift surprises his old company and meets with the silent disapproval of his old shipmaster, Captain Graveling.

In preparation for his departure from the *Rights-of-Man*, Billy goes to the lower hold to gather his gear. Meanwhile, Ratcliffe barges his way into the cabin of the *Rights-of-Man* and helps himself to a drink. Graveling plays the polite host, but refrains from drinking himself.

In a quiet moment, Graveling reproaches Ratcliffe for stealing Billy from the *Rights-of-Man*. After eliciting a meager apology, Graveling proceeds to lament his loss, recounting the tale of Billy's days on board the *Rights-of-Man*. He recalls Billy's arrival amidst a quarreling crew, the rapid rise of his popularity and authority, and his swift and judicious use of force at necessary moments. He relates a story in which a sailor referred to as "the Red Whiskers," the only member of the crew who disliked Billy, tried to bully the young sailor. When the Red Whiskers punched Billy, Billy responded with a forceful blow of his own. To the surprise of all, Billy's violent response actually pacified the Red Whiskers' hatred for Billy, turning that hatred to love. Graveling details the love felt by all for Billy the peacekeeper and dreads the encroaching discord that will doubtlessly return to the *Rights-of-Man* upon Billy's departure.

Ratcliffe delivers the tongue-in-cheek reply, "Blessed are the peacekeepers, especially the fighting peacekeepers." Then he gestures toward the cannons on board the *Bellipotent* to illustrate his idea of what a peacekeeper is. He reassures Graveling that despite the hardship of his immediate loss, he should remember that the king would doubtless approve of such selfless compliance with the needs of the empire. Calling out to Billy on deck, Ratcliffe tells him to slim down his possessions from a large box to a smaller bag.

After Billy reorganizes his gear, Ratcliffe follows him down into one of the *Bellipotent*'s cutters, or small boats, and they push off from their mooring. As they pass beneath the stern of the larger ship, Billy stands up, and, with a wave of his hat, bids a friendly good-bye to his old crew and to the *Rights-of-Man*. This last farewell earns Billy a harsh rebuke from Ratcliffe, who orders him to sit down.

SUMMARY: CHAPTER 2

> *Billy in many respects was little more than a sort of upright barbarian . . .*   (See QUOTATIONS, p. 53)

On board the *Bellipotent*, Billy quickly settles into his new routine, working good-naturedly in his position as foretopman. Markedly younger than the rest of the company, he finds himself less of a focal point among his new peers than he had been on the merchant marine. Of the other men on board the *Bellipotent*, most are far more battle-tested, although the ingenuous Billy is not intimidated by the presence of such experienced colleagues.

In passing, the narrator notes that Billy was a foundling at birth, orphaned by his parents and placed in a basket at the knocker of a stranger's door. The narrator speculates that Billy might actually be of noble parentage, given the striking quality of his appearance. Billy is depicted as a sort of natural man, chiseled and proud, but without self-consciousness. He compensates for his illiteracy with his skill as a singer. The narrator notes that Billy has a slightly bar-

baric, animal, or primitive quality in terms of his comprehension of morality. Still, Billy's only serious shortcoming is his tendency to stutter or, on occasion, to be rendered speechless. The narrator states that Billy's vocal imperfection reveals his mortality in the face of his unequaled beauty and stature. The narrator emphasizes that Billy is not a typical hero, and that his story will not be a romance.

ANALYSIS: CHAPTERS 1–2

Billy Budd is an unusual hero because he is so intellectually and emotionally limited. Throughout the novel, we are in the position of knowing and understanding more than he does. He is handsome, well liked, and widely admired, and he exhibits leadership among his fellows on the *Rights-of-Man*, but he is not gifted with unusual intelligence or self-awareness. In particular, the narrator emphasizes that although Billy exerts a good influence on other people, he lacks a well-developed moral sense. He does not have the knowledge, experience, or wisdom to be a moral role model, even though he clearly has a good heart. The narrator describes Billy by comparing him to animals and primitive men, even as he tells us that Billy is a noble specimen of manhood. Essentially, Billy Budd represents the finest qualities that nature produces in human beings without the help of civilization—he has not been cultivated by education or a sophisticated understanding of morality. The novel explores what happens when such a natural man is confronted with authority, social pressure, and the subtlety and guile of evil men.

The conflict between the individual and society is introduced relatively quickly, with Billy's impressment, or involuntary recruitment, in Chapter 1. If Billy is like man in a state of nature, as yet untroubled by the demands of civilized society, his extraction from the *Rights-of-Man* to the *Bellipotent* symbolizes the power that society exercises over individuals. The scene vividly demonstrates the idea that the demands of society overpower the rights of the individual. As the narrator points out, the *Rights-of-Man* is named after a book by Thomas Paine that defends the principles of individual liberty and human rights that inspired the French Revolution. Ironically, the *Bellipotent* removes Billy from that ship against his will, and forces him to join in the war effort against the French. The *Bellipotent* is a much more hierarchically organized and strictly run vessel, and throughout the novel it represents the forces of society and authority.

Billy's problems are greater than the conflict between an individual and an authoritarian society that strips him of his rights and freedoms. Another, more mysterious danger lies in wait for Billy—the threat of evil. The narrator introduces his view of the elusive quality of evil with the discussion of Billy's intermittent speech impediment. The narrator interprets the stutter as an indication that nature did not, in fact, make Billy perfect. He compares this imperfection to a calling card left by the devil, suggesting that the devil is fond of leaving such reminders that he has a hand in everything created on Earth, however beautiful. It is important for us to keep in mind, then, that Melville does not portray evil as a product of society, although he does not explain where it comes from or what it means. The mysterious presence of evil adds another dimension to the novel, preventing us from reducing the story to the conflict between the individual and society.

Although it is not obvious early in the novel, the first few chapters begin to establish a connection between Billy and Jesus Christ. When an officer on the *Bellipotent* asks him who his father is, Billy replies, "God knows, sir." The response indicates that Billy is simply ignorant of his origins, but it also faintly suggests that his origins are divine. Jesus was similarly evasive when asked about his parentage, and just as Billy's paternity is a mystery, the relationship between Jesus and God the Father is one of the central mysteries of Christianity. The nickname that Billy gains on board the *Bellipotent*, Baby Budd, suggests an association with the baby Jesus, aligning Billy with the Son in the Christian idea of the Holy Trinity. Several times Billy is described as "welkin-eyed"—welkin means sky—suggesting that his vision is somehow heavenly. Similar hints and references abound, but it is important not to overplay the association of Billy with Christ. After all, the differences between Billy, who is morally and spiritually limited, and Christ, who embodies divine wisdom and love, are more striking than the similarities. One of the central puzzles of *Billy Budd* is why Melville creates the parallel between Billy and Christ, and different readers have interpreted this aspect of the text in very different ways.

CHAPTERS 3–5

SUMMARY: CHAPTER 3

In these chapters, the narrator digresses from Billy's story. In Chapter 3, he discusses two major mutinies that occurred in the ranks of the British navy during the spring of 1797, the year in which Billy Budd takes place. The Great Mutiny at Nore, a sandbank in the Thames estuary that was the primary site of anchorage for the British fleet, rocked the British navy to its core. This mutiny was, according to the narrator, more menacing to the British Empire than all of the propaganda of the French Revolution and Napoleon's armies combined. Britain's navy was, after all, the right arm of the one free European power that continued to hold out in the face of Napoleon's conquest of the Continent. The "reasonable discontent" of the sailors over shoddy rations, impressment, and poor pay was ignited into an inferno by the anti-authoritarian philosophy spouted in France. But the narrator insists that rebellion against authority is not truly in the nature of British sailors, and that the mutinies were like temporary fevers that the healthy British navy soon shrugged off. Of the thousands of men who participated in the mutiny at Nore, many of them gloriously absolved themselves by their heroism at Trafalgar, where the French were defeated.

SUMMARY: CHAPTER 4

The narrator digresses further into a laudatory discussion of Admiral Sir Horatio Nelson, the national hero who commanded the British fleet at the 1805 Battle of Trafalgar. He notes that Nelson and his ship, the *Victory,* represent the last vestiges of a more poetic age, before the ugly—albeit efficient and powerful—ironclad warships of the present took over. Throughout the chapter, the narrator argues that Nelson's flashy heroism and love of glory were superior to the more technologically efficient present-day methods of war. For instance, whereas some people might be inclined to fault Nelson for sentimentally decorating himself with all of his medals and insignia before going into battle, thus making himself an easy target for the sharpshooter who killed him at Trafalgar, the narrator insists that a thirst for glory is the most important trait of a leader, and that Nelson's personal style is part of what makes him the most famous naval commander ever.

SUMMARY: CHAPTER 5

The narrator returns to a discussion of the mutinies of 1797. Although some of the mutinous sailors' demands were met, the navy could not afford to give up the practice of impressment, so naval authorities had good reason to fear that mutiny could flare up again at any time. As a result, the admiral in command of the fleet in 1797 sent Nelson, who was then a rear admiral, to command one of the ships that had recently mutinied, so that his heroic personality would galvanize the men back into loyalty.

ANALYSIS: CHAPTERS 3–5

Although Chapters 3–5 represent a departure from Billy Budd's story, they are very important in establishing the context within which the events of the novel take place. Most importantly, the fact that *Billy Budd* is set only months after the two major rebellions of 1797 would lead us to expect an atmosphere of fear to the point of paranoia on the part of the officers of Billy's ship—which, as we later see, is in fact the case. The Nore mutiny involved thousands of soldiers and struck at the heart of the British navy—not halfway around the world but within England's borders. At the time, the English had been fighting for four years to quash the French Revolution, which represented the overthrow of the monarchy and the established social order. Britain relied upon its navy to defend itself against the Revolution spreading to its shores. The widespread mutiny in the ranks of that very navy raised the specter of a homegrown revolt that could overturn British society altogether, opening the floodgates of revolution. Although the mutinies were put down, and some of the underlying causes were addressed, the navy was not able to ameliorate discontent completely because it still had to rely upon impressment to fill its ranks. Mutiny could strike again at any time.

The fact that so many of the sailors in the navy had been involuntarily impressed into service is also important in helping us understand Billy's story. Since they were there against their will, many of these men were dangerously disaffected, which explains in part the undercurrent of danger and hostility that we sense on board the *Bellipotent*. We later learn that Billy's nemesis, Claggart, whom we have yet to meet, may even have been impressed into service from a jail, given how desperate the navy is for men.

Finally, though it may be difficult for us to immediately see the relevance of the narrator's praise of Horatio Nelson, who is not a character in the novel, his example does bear on the story that we are going to read. Nelson's heroism and the glory he had accrued to his name were exploited by the navy to keep down mutiny. Though Billy's ship does not have a Horatio Nelson on board to inspire enthusiastic loyalty, Chapter 4 prepares the foundation for a comparison between Billy's captain and Nelson. Ultimately, the events of the novel are determined as much by the personalities of the men who lead as by the policies and rules that the officers claim to follow.

CHAPTERS 6–12

SUMMARY: CHAPTER 6

The narrator introduces Captain the Honorable Edward Fairfax Vere, an officer of aristocratic lineage. He is about forty years old. Though he is a highly distinguished and capable officer, there is nothing flashy about Captain Vere. He does not flaunt his nautical profession when he is onshore, and on ship he does not flaunt his authority or his rank. Beneath his modest exterior, however, he is a highly resolute man. Though practical enough when the situation calls for it, he has a tendency to lapse into a dreamy and abstracted state when not in action. He acquired the nickname "Starry Vere" after his cousin greeted him with that title upon his homecoming. The name comes from a poem by Andrew Marvell, where it refers to a military leader renowned as a severe disciplinarian.

SUMMARY: CHAPTER 7

The narrator expands upon his initial introduction of Captain Vere. A veteran of the sea, Vere has acquired certain habits over time, including a devotion to the reading of biography, history, and unconventional, common sense philosophers such as Montaigne. His penchant for reading gives him a bookish, slightly pedantic demeanor that sometimes alienates him from his fellow officers.

SUMMARY: CHAPTER 8

The narrator attempts the difficult task of describing John Claggart, the ship's master-at-arms, who functions as a sort of police captain on the vessel. In the midst of this description, the narrator explains some of the unsavory means that were employed to recruit men to ships at that time. He considers the fact that suspects and convicted criminals make up a significant portion of any given crew, especially in a time of war. While speculation abounds that Claggart himself may be a product of the prison system, the narrator dismisses this talk as idle guesswork.

SUMMARY: CHAPTER 9

> *"Baby Budd, Jemmy Legs is down on you."*
>
> (See QUOTATIONS, p. 55)

From the foretop, Billy has a bird's-eye view of the activity on the decks below. On the day after his arrival on board the *Bellipotent*, he witnesses a formal gangway punishment for the first time. After failing to show up at his assigned post, a novice suffers several lashes on his bare back, resulting in a grid of bloody welts. This incident makes a significant impression on Billy, who resolves to perform his duties diligently so as to avoid a similar beating. Nevertheless, he occasionally finds himself being censured for one minor infraction or another and feels a vague sense of threat directed toward him from his superiors.

Concerned about his predicament, Billy seeks out the Dansker, an elderly Danish mastman and seasoned veteran of the high seas. Finding him off duty on the gun deck, Billy proceeds to reveal his troubles to the Dansker, who listens attentively. After Billy finishes his tale, the Dansker volunteers his impression that Claggart, who oversees the day-to-day operations of the ship, dislikes Billy. Billy is left to puzzle over the possibility that he has fallen out of favor with Claggart, since Billy feels Claggart has spoken of him only in positive terms thus far.

SUMMARY: CHAPTER 10

The next day at lunch, Billy accidentally spills his soup on the newly scrubbed deck of the mess hall when the ship lurches. In passing, Claggart notices the accident and remarks on the handsome effect of the spill and its maker. The comment elicits a chorus of perfunctory laughter from the crew, and Billy, unable to see the sour grimace on Claggart's face when he made the comment, takes the incident as proof of Claggart's esteem for him. As Claggart continues on his way, he inadvertently bumps into a drummer boy, whom he reproves for his carelessness.

SUMMARY: CHAPTER 11

For what can more partake of the mysterious than an
antipathy spontaneous and profound. . . .
(See QUOTATIONS, p. 56)

In an aside, the narrator confirms that Claggart does, in fact, dislike Billy. The narrator can point to no rational reason for Claggart's aversion, and he suggests that to understand truly the nature of someone like Claggart, one would have to turn to the Bible for sufficiently deep insight into the human heart. Even as the narrator says this, however, he indicates that he is no great believer in the Bible, and thinks that his readers are likely to regard it as out of fashion as well. Ultimately, the narrator concludes that Claggart is simply naturally depraved. He was not corrupted by wicked books or evil influences—he was just born bad. Moreover, his depravity is especially sinister because in every outward appearance he seems rational, temperate, and free from sin. His madness cleverly hides itself deep within him.

SUMMARY: CHAPTER 12

The narrator explains that Claggart's dislike of Billy is rooted in envy. In the first place, Claggart envies Billy simply because it is his nature to be envious. He envies Billy's heroic good looks, but he also envies Billy because he can plainly see that Billy has never experienced envy or malice himself. In fact, Claggart can understand Billy's intrinsic goodness and innocence better than anyone else on the ship, and though he might like to enjoy or share in Billy's goodness, his own evil nature does not allow it. Instead, he has to play the evil role ordained for him.

ANALYSIS: CHAPTERS 6–12

Because Captain Vere is introduced right after the discussion of Horatio Nelson in Chapter 4, our attention is immediately drawn to how different Vere is from the much flashier Nelson. Although the nickname "Starry Vere" seems to suit him because of his abstracted and dreamy quality, the narrator points out that the nickname is ironic: though he is a thoroughly excellent captain, Vere does not shine. We might well be inclined to consider his modest and unassuming manner a good quality, except that the narrator has just finished explaining that the personal heroism exhibited by Nelson was an effective tool to galvanize and unite the discontented sailors. Since Vere does not lead through personal charisma, as Nelson did, we may wonder how exactly Vere will deal with the dangerously restless atmosphere in the fleet in the months following the Great Mutiny. The narrator only points to Vere's settled personal convictions. Vere leads by means of his commitment to principles, rather than by means of his personality or love of glory.

Vere's nickname is ironic in a second way, although the narrator does not point this irony out explicitly. The character referred to as "Starry Vere" in the Marvell poem is a severe disciplinarian, whereas Captain Vere is anything but harsh or brutal in his conduct. But while the name seems ironic at this point in the story, the passage quoted from the poem provides an important piece of foreshadowing. Vere does indeed impose an unexpectedly harsh discipline upon Billy, and his commitment to principle is what prompts him to be severe.

Claggart's fundamentally depraved nature is, as the narrator implies, a central component of the story. In contrast with those who have been led astray into evil ways, Claggart is simply evil beyond reasoning. The good man led astray may possibly still be rehabilitated. But the one born to evil is more difficult to understand or deal with. Even though Claggart's somewhat menacing demeanor is often attributed by his associates to his past misfortunes, the narrator asserts in no uncertain terms that Claggart is simply evil at heart. Claggart's inherently evil nature, moreover, is all the more insidious because he conceals it. The naturally depraved man, in complete possession of his faculties, may be civilized, thoroughly self-controlled, outwardly respectable, characterized by moderation, too proud to be petty, neither sensuous nor foul, and yet thoroughly evil, nonetheless. The naturally depraved man employs reason strictly in the service of irrational evil.

Thus, when Billy seeks out the Dansker in an attempt to understand his sense of foreboding, the older sailor is able to indicate a source but not a cause. The Dansker understands that Claggart's apparent friendliness toward Billy actually conceals a pernicious dislike. As hard as Billy searches for a reason behind Claggart's disapproval, he is completely at a loss for an answer. In his earnest quest to understand the situation, Billy reveals his innocence and naïveté, in contrast to the saltier, more perceptive members of the crew. In fact, in recognizing Billy's inexperience and innocence, the Dansker anoints him with the title "Baby Budd."

The respective moral natures of Billy Budd and John Claggart are symbolized by their appearances. Every bit the Handsome Sailor, Billy Budd is exactly what he appears to be: the paragon of virtue. Claggart, on the other hand, is black-haired and pale, in singular contrast to the other sailors. His visage seems "to hint of something defective or abnormal in the constitution and blood." Meanwhile, the rose-tan in Billy's cheek is seemingly lit by "the bonfire in his heart." Claggart himself reinforces the parallel between appearance and character when he cryptically remarks that "handsome is as handsome did it" in reference to the soup spill.

The narrator indicates that a clash between these polar opposites is inevitable. The discrepancy between the two, both physically and morally, inspires a hatred in Claggart that is both visceral and sustained. Most likely, Claggart finds Billy's harmlessness objectionable out of envy. In addition, although Claggart is certainly capable of recognizing and containing his complex animosity for Billy, he can hardly overcome it. Thus, within the confines of the warship, the simmering conflict between Claggart and Billy seems destined to continue brewing until it boils over.

CHAPTERS 13–17

SUMMARY: CHAPTER 13

The narrator explains that profound passions can exist in the lowliest settings, and may be provoked by trivial circumstances. The passion to which he refers belongs to Claggart, who is beginning to resent Billy with fervent intensity. Given time to reflect upon the matter, Claggart arrives at the conclusion that Billy's soup spill is no accident. Rather, he believes that it is a gesture revealing Billy's ill will toward him, whether this antagonism is conscious or not. Squeak, a wizened corporal and Claggart's underling, who also has it in for Billy, reinforces Claggart's opinions. In addition to persecuting Billy at every opportunity, Squeak lies to Claggart and tells him that Billy makes fun of him behind his back. Searching for a reason to justify his hatred of Billy and encouraged by Squeak's lies, Claggart seizes upon the soup spill as an indication of Billy's malice and uses it as an excuse to increase the level of his own enmity.

SUMMARY: CHAPTER 14

Shortly thereafter, on a warm night, Billy inadvertently becomes involved in a troubling incident. While dozing on an upper deck of the ship, he is roused by a whisper and a touch to his shoulder. An anonymous figure tells Billy to meet him shortly thereafter on a narrow balcony in a remote part of the ship. Innocently, Billy gets up mechanically and goes to the balcony as instructed. Presently, the other man arrives, and though it is dark and hazy Billy is able to identify him as one of the afterguardsmen. Declaring that he was forced into duty just like Billy, the man asks Billy in a roundabout way if he would be willing to assist, if ever a mutiny occurred.

Not immediately grasping the man's meaning, Billy presses him for a further explanation. When the man holds up a pair of coins and declares them to be Billy's for the taking, Billy reacts violently, stuttering in fits and starts. Billy orders the man to return to his place on the ship, threatening to throw him overboard if he does not comply. Taking Billy for his word, the man scuttles off. Awakened by Billy's loud threat and knowing that Billy stutters only when something is truly amiss, a forecastleman emerges to check on the commotion. Billy explains that he has sent a trespassing afterguardsman back to his proper place on the ship. At this, yet another forecastleman comes forth, this time to rebuke Billy for his relative mildness in dealing with the encroaching afterguardsman. However, Billy convinces the forecastlemen that everything has been handled with adequate gruffness, and the matter is dropped.

SUMMARY: CHAPTER 15

In the aftermath of this incident, Billy wrestles with his conscience, as he has no prior experience in the world of the corrupt or the illicit. He is at a loss to explain the nature of the afterguardsman's bribe or to figure out where the afterguardsman might have acquired guineas at sea. The more he considers the matter, the more bewildered he becomes. At the very least, Billy perceives that the whole affair smacks of evil. Therefore, he decides that he has no wish to be associated with it, although he is curious to learn more of its specific nature.

The following afternoon, Billy spots the man he thinks to be the afterguardsman on an upper gun deck. The man on the gun deck hardly fits the picture of a jaded conspirator, however. The man spots Billy before Billy spots him, and sends a nod in Billy's direction. A couple of days later, the two men again cross paths on a gun deck, and the afterguardsman offers a friendly but unexpected word of greeting to Billy. Embarrassed by the awkward situation, Billy fails to return the greeting and is sent into a greater confusion by the odd turn of events.

Once again, Billy chooses to unburden himself to the salty old Dansker. After hearing Billy's heavily generalized version of his encounters, the Dansker concludes for a second time that Claggart is out to get him. Billy, taken aback by such an interpretation, presses the Dansker for an explanation, but the Dansker simply retreats into mysterious silence.

SUMMARY: CHAPTER 16
Despite the Dansker's repeated warning, Billy refuses to suspect Claggart of foul play. The narrator explains that sailors are, as a rule, immature to the point of being juvenile, and Billy, in his relative inexperience, is no exception. But even the little experience that Billy does have has hardly made him any less innocent, because he so completely lacks the inner impulse toward badness that would help him to understand it. The narrator returns to the idea that sailors are in general an innocent and unsophisticated group, and notes that in life on land, most people learn to distrust one another. This distrust is so taken for granted that most people would be quite surprised if it were pointed it out to them.

SUMMARY: CHAPTER 17
While the random persecution of Billy abates for the moment, Claggart maintains his hatred toward Billy. In general, Claggart presents a façade of good-humored amity toward Billy, but when his guard is down, his enmity flashes forth visibly in his eyes. Billy, however, remains completely oblivious to Claggart's hatred, taking the latter's kind words toward him at face value. The narrator notes that due to Billy's genial nature and his general popularity, he is less perceptive of ill will than the usual sailor. Thus, he fails to notice when the armorer and the captain of the hold, two officers associated with Claggart, begin to regard him with malice and suspicion.

ANALYSIS: CHAPTERS 13–17
With the narrator's talk of stages and "groundlings" at the beginning of Chapter 13, Melville signals to us that he is invoking his favorite literary influence—the plays of Shakespeare. He does not

mention Shakespeare or Shakespeare's characters by name, but in the final paragraph of the chapter he borrows phrases from Shakespeare's *Othello* no fewer than five times—"injury but suspected," "monstrous disproportion," "an inordinate usurer," "lawyer to his will," and "ogres of trifles" are all quotations from that play. Clearly, Melville wants to associate Claggart with the villain Iago, and the two characters do share many traits. Like Claggart, Iago nurses a passionate and sustained hatred that he successfully hides from the outer world. He claims to be motivated by envy, and though envy is definitely a part of his psychological makeup, the depths of his malice defy easy explanation. By associating Claggart with this character from a Shakespearean tragedy, Melville seeks to portray Claggart as larger than life, while bearing out his own claim that grand and tragic passions occur among lowly people just as much as within the inner circles of the powerful.

Claggart's passion is a kind of paranoia—or, as the narrator labels it, a monomania, meaning an obsession with a single idea. As Captain Ahab demonstrates in Melville's *Moby-Dick,* paranoia and monomania are closely related. Because Claggart has become obsessed with his hatred of Billy, he willfully interprets the spilled soup as Billy's hostile response to his own animosity. The fundamental evil in Claggart cannot rest. Claggart is enslaved to his own evil ideas, driven ceaselessly in pursuit of selfish ends and looking for any possible opening to convince himself that his hatred for Billy is justified and necessary. While Billy's actions may be trivial—and in the case of the soup, unintentional—Claggart's skewed interpretation misrepresents Billy's motivations.

The afterguardsman's nighttime attempt to corrupt Billy may not be what it seems. The narrator alludes earlier to traps set for sailors by Claggart and Squeak, and this could well be one of them. Whatever the afterguardsman's true motives, Billy gets his first glimpse of the darker side of man in his night-time encounter with this man, but his innocence keeps him from gaining a clear grasp of the fact that the man is asking him to be disloyal. Billy has a general sense of foreboding from the meeting, but he is so inexperienced that he is unable to pin it down as a call to mutiny. Therefore, with only a vague notion of any potential underhanded activities, Billy never thinks to report the event, even though he remarks upon its "extreme questionableness." The afterguardsman's attempt to entrap Billy is foiled by Billy's naïve innocence. Yet even if Billy had gained a better understanding of the conspiratorial proceedings, the narrator speculates that Billy would have applied his "novice magnanimity" to the situation and refused to play the role of a snitch. In using the word "novice" to describe Billy's "magnanimity," the narrator strikes an ironic note, suggesting that the schoolyard honor code of silence is a more primitive and underdeveloped form of that which is truly moral. By implication, the truer magnanimity would be to root out the evil conspiracy before it spreads and strikes. Billy, however, blinded by his own innocence, cannot decipher this moral quandary.

Melville suggests that we must come to recognize evil but also implies that those who have come to know it are often taught, or teach themselves, to shrink back from it. The narrator describes an "undemonstrative distrustfulness" that pervades the deeper affairs between men who recognize the reality of natural depravity. Even though he sees Billy's ignorance, the Dansker refrains from speaking out against the evil. The narrator attributes his silence to a "long experience," which had led him to "that bitter prudence which never interferes ... and never gives advice." Over the course of his life, the Dansker has become so "bitter" that he will not speak out against evil when he recognizes it. The narrator indicates that the Dansker's cynicism stems from his experience with "superiors," implying that the Dansker's passivity stems from a deep-rooted impulse to avoid further conflict with authority. Should his prediction be wrong, or should Claggart find out about his statements, the Dansker knows all too well how he would fare.

Thus, if those who cannot recognize evil are unequipped to fight it, and those who are aware of evil choose not to fight it, a depraved world where evil is simply left to its own devices inevitably results. Man, and especially man on land, eventually learns from experience that social life, in its gridlock of mistrust, becomes "an oblique, tedious, barren game hardly worth that poor candle burned out in playing it." In the narrator's view, the impossibility of mutual trust seems to rob life on land of all savor and meaning. Moreover, as the example of the Dansker shows, potentially beneficial warnings often remain unvoiced and hidden between so-called well-meaning men, casting an even more depressing shadow over human existence. This breakdown of communication is not only complete, but also unacknowledged and unconscious. After all, the narrator concedes that he is merely speculating when he states that life experience "had very likely" driven the Dansker to withhold his advice. Despite his apparent omniscience elsewhere in the story, the narrator does not speak with an authoritative tone here, perhaps because Melville wishes to emphasize the impenetrable nature of the problems associated with evil and its perpetuation among men.

CHAPTERS 18–19

SUMMARY: CHAPTER 18

Away from the fleet on a mission, the *Bellipotent* encounters an enemy frigate, which, outsized by the *Bellipotent,* turns sail and flees. After some pursuit, the enemy escapes, and the *Bellipotent* abandons chase. As the excitement subsides on board, Claggart approaches the mainmast to obtain an interview with Captain Vere. Such a request is unusual, and Vere is taken aback by the appearance of this unfamiliar officer, who inspires a vague unease in him.

Claggart proceeds to reveal his suspicion that a mutiny conspiracy may be fomenting among a group of impressed men on the gun decks, alluding to the Nore mutiny in order to further alarm the captain . Vere, unsettled by such a report, is also disturbed by Claggart's demeanor as he relates this information. Vere mulls over the implications of potential insubordination in his ranks, taking note of Claggart's lack of tact in bringing up the sensitive issue of the Nore mutiny and his immodest, forward testimony.

Vere, wishing to bring things to a point, asks Claggart to identify his prime suspect. Claggart responds by naming William (Billy) Budd, a foretopman. Truly surprised by this assertion, Vere notes that Billy is so roundly liked by the crew that they call him the Handsome Sailor. Claggart explains that Billy creates an aura of friendliness so that his shipmates will defend him in a pinch, and insists that his genial demeanor masks a sinister nature. Vere, reflecting on his approval of Billy's conduct thus far and his enthusiasm for having such a young and capable sailor, grows increasingly suspicious of Claggart's motives.

When Vere demands that Claggart produce a piece of evidence to support his claim against Billy, Claggart responds with a series of further accusations that he claims he can prove. Vere prepares to demand such proof but thinks twice about it, deciding to be more discreet instead. Therefore, he sends a boy to bring Billy to the captain's cabin without revealing where they are going. Meanwhile, he dismisses Claggart to a lower deck, telling him to return to the cabin when Billy arrives.

SUMMARY: CHAPTER 19

Billy arrives and sits with Claggart and Vere in the confines of the cabin. Vere directs Claggart to confront Billy with his accusation. Claggart speaks with great precision, rendering Billy speechless, stunning him completely. Vere demands that Billy speak up to defend himself, but Billy remains tongue-tied. Noticing Billy's tendency to stutter and be mute, Vere softens his approach, telling Billy to take his time in formulating a response. These encouraging words only throw Billy further into a fury, as he wrenches his body into a contortion, still unable to reply.

Suddenly, in a moment of impulse, Billy strikes Claggart a blow to the forehead, knocking him over. Claggart lets out a brief gasp upon hitting the ground and then lies motionless. Vere, as though shocked, softly bewails this ill-fated turn, and directs Billy to help him raise Claggart off the ground. They slouch him up into a sitting position and then lay him down again. Vere dismisses Billy to a nearby stateroom and summons the ship's surgeon to the cabin.

The surgeon arrives to find Claggart prostrate and bleeding from the nose and ears. A swift check confirms the worst, and Claggart is pronounced dead. Suddenly, Vere grasps the surgeon's arm and declares Claggart's death to be a divine judgment, visited upon him by an angel. In the same breath, he exclaims that the angel, nevertheless, must be hanged. Lacking knowledge about the context of Claggart's death, the surgeon is quite concerned by the captain's mysterious agitation. Slowly, Vere collects himself and explains the affair briefly to the surgeon. He then enlists him to help remove Claggart's body from the cabin. Once this is accomplished, Vere directs the surgeon to inform the lieutenants and the marine captain of the incident, but otherwise to keep the affair secret. Though somewhat disturbed by this clandestine air, the subordinate surgeon has no choice but to carry out the captain's orders.

ANALYSIS: CHAPTERS 18–19

Finally, with Claggart's bold accusation and Billy's emboldened defense, the narrative springs to life and reaches its climax. The blow that Billy strikes may seem uncharacteristic, but his resort to violence in a moment of speechlessness is not without precedent. Captain Graveling, Billy's superior on the *Rights-of-Man,* relates the romantic tale of Billy and the Red Whiskers in the very first chapter of the story. The incident with the Red Whiskers functions as a foreshadowing of Billy's confrontation with Claggart. Melville's name choice for the Red Whiskers is doubtless calculated to remind us of the devil, and the Red Whiskers is similar to Claggart in a number of significant ways. Like Claggart, the Red Whiskers dislikes Billy, and out of sheer envy he "bestirs" himself to pick a fight with Billy.

However, Billy actually pacifies the Red Whiskers with his blows, whereas his violence toward Claggart is fatal. Thus, Billy's encounter with Claggart ends not in reconciliation but in Billy's fall from grace. The narrator depicts this fall in explicitly religious images, noting for instance that as Billy struggles to reply to Claggart's accusation, his expression is like the face of a man being crucified. Billy lashes out impulsively against his false accuser, and as Billy and Vere struggle to sit Claggart's body up, the narrator notes that the sensation of handling the corpse is "like handling a dead snake." With these words, Claggart's role as the serpent, or Satan, becomes more explicit. Similar biblical imagery has been present throughout the story, however, and it is important to recognize that Claggart is not the only person or thing associated with Satan. Certainly, the Red Whiskers appears devilish and evil if for no other reason than the suggestive color in his title. The narrator suggests in the early chapters that Billy's speech impediment exemplifies the serpent's inescapable evil influence. Billy comes face-to-face with evil in the captain's cabin, but Melville takes care to show us that evil is not limited to Claggart's person, but is spread throughout creation.

Vere makes a different biblical allusion when he labels Claggart's unforeseen death "the divine judgment on Ananias." Vere refers here to a biblical story from the Acts of the Apostles, in which a man named Ananias attempts to take credit for more than he deserves but drops dead upon being found out by Peter, who rebukes him by saying, "You have lied not to human beings, but to God" (Acts 5:4). Vere associates this gross deception with Claggart, who in his depravity has exceeded all bounds of propriety with his lies. Even though Billy appears angelic in the story, and even though Vere declares that Billy represents the angel sent by God to strike down Claggart, Vere nevertheless exclaims, "Yet the angel must hang!" Vere's exclamation expresses his frustrated realization about how Billy will be viewed in the eyes of the military law.

Melville's narrator challenges us to judge Vere's judgment of Billy. Each person, he suggests, "must determine for himself by such light as this narrative affords" whether Captain Vere was really "the sudden victim of any degree of aberration"—in other words, whether he was a victim of temporary insanity. Vere's insistence on procedure accords with his abstract, intellectual, starry bent. As Vere already appears aloof and detached in the eyes of many of his peers, his decision to proceed with the prosecution at once seems to many a rash, perhaps slightly crazy decision. But Vere does have reasons to support his decision—any show of hesitation in punishing the killing of an officer will send a dangerous message to the crew. Melville's narrator, in taking up the question of Vere's sanity, declares that no such decisive division between sanity and insanity exists. The narrator insists that no observer can truly distinguish between sanity and insanity, although there will always be certain medical charlatans who will claim to be able to do so for the right amount of money.

CHAPTERS 20–21

SUMMARY: CHAPTER 20

> *"Struck dead by an angel of God! Yet the angel*
> *must hang!"*   (See QUOTATIONS, p. 58)

Plagued by doubts about Vere's state of mind, the surgeon exits the cabin. He considers Vere's impending prosecution of the affair a rash move and thinks that a more sensible course would be to detain Billy until the case can be referred to the admiral. However, the surgeon's low rank prevents him from arguing with Vere's wishes, and he carries out orders without so much as a single word. Upon hearing of Claggart's death, the lieutenants and captains share the same dismay at Vere's hasty prosecution of Billy. Each one concludes independently that any trial would be better reserved for the judgment of the admiral.

SUMMARY: CHAPTER 21

Nevertheless, in order to circumvent any potential mutinous activity that might develop when Billy's plight becomes public, Vere resolves to keep the matter secret and to act on it quickly. He appoints a small drumhead court consisting of the first lieutenant, the captain of marines, and the sailing master; without further delay, Billy's arraignment proceeds. As sole witness, Vere relates the events of the day to the court, detailing Claggart's accusations against Billy, and Billy's reaction to Claggart. When the first lieutenant asks Billy to corroborate Vere's account, he does so but denies the truth of Claggart's accusations. Vere responds to Billy's claim with a vote of confidence, and Billy thanks the captain graciously, almost breaking down in a fit of emotion.

Upon being questioned about his relations with Claggart, Billy recovers himself, explaining that there was no malice between them. He declares that he had not meant to kill Claggart, but that in reaction to Claggart's lies in the presence of the captain and without the ability to explain verbally, his only defense was to strike a blow. The court next asks Billy about any knowledge he may have had regarding a potential conspiracy. After hesitating, Billy decides to declare that he has no such knowledge. Interpreting his pause as a function of his condition, the court is satisfied with his response.

Finally, the court asks Billy why Claggart invented a lie against him if no malice existed between them. The narrator explains that Billy is unable to muster an answer due to the spiritual nature of the question. Billy looks to Vere for assistance and Vere rises, declaring that the only person who could answer such a question is the dead man, Claggart himself. Moreover, Vere declares that the question is not relevant, explaining that the matter at hand is to judge the pertinent actions and their consequences, regardless of their causes, motives, or intentions. This formula inspires a deep-seated sense of surprise in both Billy and in the court. When the court presses for a more complete understanding of the context in which Claggart accused Billy—and by extension, of the context in which Billy struck Claggart—Vere once again dismisses the court's wish. He argues that such contextual information is irrelevant to the question of guilt or innocence with regard to Billy's deed.

Not entirely understanding the import of Captain Vere's words, Billy sits silently in the aftermath of Vere's declaration. Vere shoots an authoritative look in the direction of the first lieutenant, who then asks Billy if he has anything else to say in his defense. After a quick glance at Vere, Billy announces that he has nothing left to say. With this, Billy is removed from the courtroom and escorted back to the stateroom where he was initially detained. As the adjudicators silently deliberate, Vere turns his back on their proceedings, gazing out of a porthole upon the sea and later pacing back and forth in the cabin.

Shortly thereafter, Vere confronts the adjudicators, declaring that he would have been content to remain simply in the role of a witness

SUMMARY & ANALYSIS

had it not been for their reluctance to make a decision. He reminds them of their practical, military duty and implores them to place their responsibilities to the law of the kingdom above any reservations they may feel within their individual consciences. His argument only serves to agitate the judges further, and an emotional debate ensues between Vere and the officer of marines regarding the wide gulf between the effects of Billy's actions and the nature of his intentions.

Concluding his remarks on the wartime imperative to observe the rule of law absolutely, Vere demands swift and decisive action by the court, either to acquit or to condemn. The sailing master proposes to convict but to lessen the penalty, an alternative that Vere dismisses as damaging to the integrity of authority and discipline on board the *Bellipotent* and potentially leading to mutiny. With this, Vere returns to the porthole to contemplate the sea once more, leaving the adjudicators to make a decision. The adjudicators decide to convict Billy Budd and sentence him to death by hanging at dawn.

Analysis: Chapters 20–21

Vere's decisions in these chapters represent the heart of *Billy Budd*, because the central moral problem posed by this novel is the question of what the just response to Billy's crime would be. Vere, notwithstanding his sophisticated grasp of the complexity of the situation, is never truly in doubt about what must happen to Billy. He has known from the moment he witnessed Billy strike Claggart dead that Billy has to hang. In these chapters, Vere plays the part of Pontius Pilate to Billy's Jesus, because Vere refuses to use his authority to do what he thinks is right, just as Pilate washes his hands of the question of Jesus' fate. (Pontius Pilate was the Roman governor of Judaea—from 26 BC to 36 BC—responsible for the execution of Jesus of Nazareth.) But if Vere plays Pilate's role, he does not do so by abdicating responsibility for making a decision—if anything, he is even more aware than Pilate of the consequences of his actions. His summoning of the drumhead court is not intended as a way to shift the responsibility for the decision away from himself, because he knows that the court will defer to his judgment. Vere's proceedings are all calculated to create the appearance of due process and fairness for the benefit of the crew—the outcome, however, is never in question.

Vere knows that Billy must be executed quickly. Otherwise, regardless of the extenuating circumstances, the rest of the crew will only understand that Billy killed his superior officer and got away with it. Consequently, the crew will either be outraged that mutiny was treated with such unfair lenience, or tempted to similar action because of Billy's success, or both. Moreover, Vere does not bend the law at all in his strict instructions to the court. The Mutiny Act, under which Billy is condemned, was implemented precisely in order to deter mutiny by punishing any act of violence against a superior officer with death, no matter what the circumstances. Vere upholds the spirit as well as the letter of this law, and if we feel that the outcome in this case is unjust, as we probably do, then we have to consider why the Mutiny Act itself is unjust.

Vere provides all the clues to what is wrong about executing Billy. In the first place, he says that God would certainly acquit Billy, and no doubt will do so on judgment day, but that naval officers are forced to set aside considerations of God's law in rendering a decision according to military law. Furthermore, the decision that Vere urges upon his reluctant subordinates clearly violates own conscience, every bit as much as theirs. Vere feels that Billy is fundamentally innocent, even angelic, and when he visits Billy to inform him of the verdict, he seems to feel that he owes Billy something, both as a friend and as a fellow human being, that conflicts with his duties as a captain. Apparently Vere feels that his duty as a soldier is at odds with God, morality, and his own conscience—all of which oppose the sacrifice of an individual life for the sake of another end, in this case, the security and success of the British navy.

Ultimately, Vere makes plain that judging Billy under the Mutiny Act is no different from killing an enemy soldier in a war. In war, the soldiers on one side will kill those of the other side, even if they were forced into service against their will, and perhaps even sympathize with the cause against which they are forced to fight. The essence of war is to sacrifice individual lives in the service of larger ends, and as Vere sees it, that is what has happened to Billy as well. What Melville tries to show through the case of Billy Budd is that waging war requires a nation to be as brutal to its own subjects as it is to its enemies. It is worth noting, in this context, that military law is very different in principle from civilian law. There are many different views of what laws are and what they mean, but one way to view law is as the embodiment of principles of justice, and when courts apply a law in a particular case, they seek to bring about a just outcome. Whether or not this is true of civilian law, it is clearly not true of military law, particularly not in the case of the Mutiny Act.

CHAPTERS 22–25

SUMMARY: CHAPTER 22

Vere announces the sentence directly to Billy in his stateroom prison. Further details of their interview remain unknown, although the narrator imagines a frank and open exchange in which Vere explains all and Billy nobly accepts his explanation. As Vere exits the stateroom, the first lieutenant perceives—quite to his surprise—a look of extreme anguish on the captain's face.

SUMMARY: CHAPTER 23

In the past hour and a half, while Billy, Claggart, and Vere were still in the cabin, speculation about the situation has run rampant among the ship's company. Now, Vere's explanation to the crew is direct and precise. He recounts the events of the evening, announces the impending execution, and foregoes all elaboration and further explanation. The sailors listen in silence for much of the announcement, and a mounting murmur at its conclusion is quickly stifled by orders to resume normal duties. Thereafter, Claggart receives a formal burial at sea with little fanfare, but in perfect accordance with military custom. Meanwhile, Billy remains held in irons until dawn, watched over by a sentry, and denied all communication except with the chaplain.

SUMMARY: CHAPTER 24

Shackled and guarded, placed in a gun bay, and dressed in his dirty white sailor's suit, Billy stands in stark contrast to the dark machinery that envelops him. While he maintains his rosy complexion, signs of emaciation begin to show in his cheeks as he awaits his execution. With his fate sealed, his agony has largely dissipated, and his relaxed posture embodies one concentrated in the repose of memory.

The chaplain, happening upon Billy in this state of tranquility, withdraws without disturbing him. Later in the night, the chaplain returns to find Billy awake. Billy welcomes the chaplain to his side, and, during their ensuing discussion, the chaplain attempts to prepare Billy for the death that awaits him. Billy listens to the chaplain with polite attentiveness, but as both the narrator and the chaplain note, he seems to be in a state of grace and aware of his own innocence, and does not fear death. In fact, due to his morally primitive nature, Billy is by no means awed by the chaplain's Christian message, but is instead politely respectful, as toward a gift that he cannot really understand. When the chaplain realizes that Billy does not fear death, he decides that innocence is as good a state as penitence in which to greet one's maker, and he prepares to leave. Before departing, the chaplain kisses Billy on the cheek.

SUMMARY: CHAPTER 25

At 4 A.M., the first light of dawn appears. Whistles ring out around the ship, summoning all hands forward to witness the hanging. From various parts of the ship, the sailors gather to watch the events in the main yard, where Vere commands attention, and Billy is presently brought forth by the chaplain. After a brief blessing, the chaplain withdraws. Just prior to his ultimate moment, Billy declares, "God bless Captain Vere!" The assembled sailors echo his sentiment, seemingly involuntarily. Vere exhibits no reaction to this turn of events, and in the next instant, Billy's execution proceeds as planned. Dawn breaks as Billy expires and is left to hang, shifting softly and lifelessly with the motion of the rolling ship.

ANALYSIS: CHAPTERS 22–25

Billy's story becomes more and more specifically intertwined with religion as the novel nears its close. With the trial concluded and Billy's fate sealed, Vere now shifts gears back from captain to friend when he informs Billy of the court's decision. Though Melville elects not to include the precise details of their conversation, he does offer up another biblical allusion. Because of Vere's dual role as a father figure and a devotee of the law, Melville compares him to Abraham, who was called upon by God to sacrifice his only son, Isaac. Though reluctant to face this test, Abraham carried out God's wishes, placing his belief in God's decree above his own individual conscience. In a similar way, Vere places his duty to martial law above his own sense of duty to Billy Budd, sacrificing him to war. There is unquestionably a profound irony to all the parallels between the Bible and Billy's fate, since, as Vere has already pointed out to us, Billy is not being sacrificed to God, but in direct opposition to the dictates of religion.

With Billy in chains and guarded by a sentry, there is a profound incongruity in the presence of a chaplain, who ostensibly represents Jesus, the prophet of forgiveness, meekness, and mercy. Emphasizing this irony, Melville describes the chaplain as "the minister of the Prince of Peace serving in the host of the God of War"—a man of the cloth who nevertheless "receives his stipend from Mars," meaning that he is fed and paid by the navy, not the church. The warship employs the chaplain to place the ethical seal of approval on that which is "the abrogation of everything but brute force." Religion does not transcend the state of war, but instead has to subordinate itself to "the discipline and purposes of war."

The chaplain himself is quite powerless to change Billy's fate. He is well aware of his subordinate role on board the warship, and knows that he is in no position to put his Christian code of morality above the commands of the officers. As such, he has to modify his convictions as the circumstances of war and naval discipline demand, comforting himself with the thought that Billy's innocence will serve him well at Judgment, even if it cannot save him here on Earth. In any event, the chaplain's discussion of salvation is lost on Billy, who receives his abstract talk more out of simple politeness than out of awe or reverence. And, sensing Billy's good heart, the chaplain is content to leave it at that, withdrawing with a secular kiss of benediction before parting. The merging of religion with war is not specific to *Billy Budd* but, in fact, can be seen throughout history. The Christian religion itself did not begin to spread in earnest until it was adopted by bellicose Roman emperors such as Constantine and Theodosius in the fourth century A.D. Similarly, organized religions have survived and flourished thanks to their military might. Upon close examination, the line in such cultural traditions begins to blur, leading us to question whether religion advances war or war advances religion.

In these chapters, Vere becomes the quintessential representative of the cold power of war. Even though the narrator notes Vere's potential shock when Billy praises him while being strung up to the gallows, Vere remains the very image of military power. He is resembles "a musket in the ship armorer's rack," standing at attention without flinching. Like the ship's chaplain, Vere does not feel completely comfortable in the role set out for him, but he nevertheless remains steadfast in his position as captain throughout the proceedings, sacrificing Billy as a "Lamb of God" to the greater good.

Outshining both the chaplain and Vere, however, Billy flourishes in his final sacrificial role. Indeed, from Billy's initial stutter down to his last breath, the details of his final day and night recall the last days of Jesus. The Passion traditionally refers to the story of the suffering and death of Christ, and the narrator's tale appears like the denouement of what could be called Billy's Passion. Billy's agony upon being accused was "as a crucifixion to behold," and through his silence and shame until his death, he strikes a most familiar pose, right down to the sense of a resurrection. At the moment that Billy expires, the dawn breaks dramatically, and in an unusual and remarkable twist, Billy is free from the convulsions that normally accompany death on the gallows.

However, as the narrator clearly shows, Billy dies not as a Christian, but more vaguely as a spiritual man. Billy's cryptic final blessing seems almost divine in its patient understanding of Vere, nearly outdoing even the repose of Jesus upon the cross, who questioned rather than praised his father. The narrator establishes that Billy welcomed the chaplain but he did not adapt to the chaplain's particularly Christian advances. Instead, Billy was "spiritualized" in the end. As before, Billy appears to be connected to a more primitive, innocent, and childlike nature, but here the narrator shows that Billy's simplicity is a spiritual alternative to Christian theology, not an abrogation of spirituality itself.

Chapters 26–30

Summary: Chapter 26
Leaping forward a few days, the ship's purser and surgeon discuss the strange fact that Billy's body dangled from his execution rope with preternatural tranquility in the moments after he was hanged. The purser wonders aloud why Billy failed to convulse under the pressure of being hanged and chooses to attribute this unusual placidity to some sort of willpower within Billy. Meanwhile, the surgeon, committed to the principles of science, is unable to account for the phenomenon but unwilling to assign it a supernatural cause. Dismissing the purser's speculations about Billy's death as inauthentic, the surgeon abruptly takes his leave to attend to a patient in the sick bay.

Summary: Chapter 27
In the silence that follows Billy's execution, a low murmur emerges from the ship's company. Slightly foreboding in nature, it is a murmur that has no chance of gathering steam. In the next moment, the whistles ring out once again to restore normalcy, and the sailors' superiors command them to return to their duties. After the last preparations for burial are made, all hands are called to gather

again, and Billy is laid to rest at sea. As the corpse settles, another murmur rises from the crew, and they watch as a flock of birds circles the spot where the burial has just occurred. The men observe this event with fascinated contemplation, lingering briefly until yet another call to quarters sends the crew back to their duties. As the sailors disperse, the various lieutenants salute in turn and present their final report to the captain. By Vere's command, the regular day begins earlier than usual, with a brief prayer service followed by the return of the men to their various perches.

SUMMARY: CHAPTER 28

The narrator states that his narrative has more to do with fact than with fiction, and as a result, it will not have a clean, symmetrical ending. He says that faithfully told truths always feel unfinished. He draws attention to the fact that, with Billy's death, the main part of his story has been concluded, but that the last three chapters will serve as a sequel.

Later on the same voyage, the *Bellipotent* engages in battle with the French battleship *Athée*, or *Atheist*. During the fighting, Vere is struck by an enemy musket ball and carried below the deck. Under the command of the senior lieutenant, the *Bellipotent* captures the *Athée* and brings the enemy into port at Gibraltar. Vere, laid up with the wounded, dies shortly thereafter. An attendant recalls that, as Vere lay on his deathbed, he murmured the words, "Billy Budd, Billy Budd."

SUMMARY: CHAPTER 29

A few weeks after Claggart's death and Billy's execution, news of the incident appears in a naval chronicle. The report describes the supposed conspiracy led by "one William Budd," who turned upon his accuser, Claggart, and "vindictively stabbed him in the heart." A general editorial follows this misinformation, eulogizing the innocent Claggart and condemning the villainous Budd. The narrator notes that this report is the only surviving official record of the incident or of the respective characters of John Claggart and Billy Budd.

SUMMARY: CHAPTER 30

In the years that follow Billy Budd's tragic ending, his legend begins to grow. The spar from which he was hanged is followed from port to port and venerated by many in the manner of the Christian cross. As his reputation continues to spread, another foretopman composes some lines in his memory. After circulating among the naval ranks for a while, these lines are printed in ballad form at an English publishing house. The poem, entitled "Billy in the Darbies," is a sympathetic literary recreation of Billy Budd's last hours in the ship's hold. With this denouement, the narrator withdraws back into the shadows of the deep, along with Billy Budd.

ANALYSIS: CHAPTERS 26–30

Melville has already shown that the chaplain's religion must subordinate itself to the power of war, and here his narrator describes the absolute example of the cold and spiritless nature of warfare. The *Bellipotent* meets its match in the French war ship *Athée,* or *Atheist.* Such a title of "infidel audacity" is, to the narrator, "the aptest name, if one consider it, ever given to a warship," thus implying that all warships, regardless of nationality, are dedicated to an essentially godless pursuit. It is this infidel power to which Vere eventually succumbs, with the name of the innocent Billy Budd on his lips as he breathes his last.

Captain Vere's death scene recalls Chapter 4, where the narrator reveres Captain Nelson for his spiritual, sentimental nature. Despite Nelson's victory at Trafalgar, the narrator's contemporaries disparage Nelson and ridicule him for his vainglorious qualities, indicating a shift to a colder and darker conception of war, more powerful but less human. Here again, the irreverent war machine continues to kill off the more honorable, spiritual captains in the name of power and success. More important, however, war takes not only the captain as sacrifice, but the Handsome Sailor too. While introducing Vere's scene with the *Athée,* the narrator indicates that he has already shown "how it fared with the Handsome Sailor during the year of the Great Mutiny." Ominously, the narrator refers not just to the death of Billy Budd the individual man, but to the death of the Handsome Sailor ideal itself, sacrificed on the alter of the Mutiny Act and the war gods.

Despite the ambiguous circumstances of Billy's condemnation and death, however, the narrator shows that his legend will grow among naval circles, lending support to the lesson that actions themselves override the intentions and motives behind them, whether good or bad. The military newspaper clearly has the wrong story, but the narrator also shows that those who venerate the sparpiece of Billy's execution "as a piece of the Cross" do not have the story straight either. Over the succeeding days and months, Billy's legend is transformed into an indisputable narrative, much in the fashion that Jesus' legend slowly solidified among the apostles of what eventually became the early Christian church. In this way, a scriptural hodgepodge, rather than the true words and actions of Billy Budd, becomes the object of worship and veneration. Like John, Luke, Mark, Matthew, and, most of all, Paul, the anonymous foretopman acts as a secondhand chronicler, and the words of his poem become conflated with Billy's actual fate, just as the Gospels and Epistles presume to speak for Jesus.

Taking up the theme of a possible resurrection, Melville creates a scene of dispute between the believer and the doubter in the forms of the ship's purser and surgeon. The purser, noting the odd circumstances of Billy's death, chances to ascribe some supernatural power to his passing. As a scientist, the surgeon dismisses any such notion, refusing to believe in the individual's power to transcend nature. Moreover, Melville's opinion in the resurrection debate lies with the scientific surgeon. The narrator describes the purser as "more accurate as an accountant than profound as a philosopher." In addition, references to Billy as a man with a profound connection to primitive nature abound in the work, and resonate with the surgeon's interpretation of his death. The final lines of the final poem situate Billy in the weeds at the bottom of the ocean, not resurrected in heaven.

This does not mean, however, that Melville *prefers* to look at the world in such a scientific way. Rather, like the surgeon, Melville and his narrator depart at the end of the book in a vague and somewhat unsatisfactory fashion, leaving an ambiguous poem to sum up the tale. In the scene with the purser, the surgeon departs quickly but uneasily. He sharply cuts off his dialogue with the purser prior to coming to any agreement or conclusion, preferring to rest on the foundations of science than to risk delving into an unknown and potentially treacherous subject for him. Similarly, Melville retreats like the surgeon, recognizing only what he can see: the pervasive nature of evil among mankind and the powerlessness of the so-called redemptive Christian tradition in the face of such evil.

To his credit, Melville's narrator warns his readership that the story will not tie up in a clean fashion. Thus, in concluding with the final poem, *Billy Budd* spirals into a web of indeterminate authorship, intention, and verity. Billy's story, the narrator concludes, always appears in skewed terms from secondhand sources and should never receive the blind trust that so many so freely offer it.

Thus, it is fitting that in closing the story of Billy Budd, the narrator relates that "the general estimate of his nature ... found rude utterance from another foretopman" gifted "with an artless *poetic* temperament." The emphasis on "poetic" suggests the poem suffers from unavoidable embellishment—unavoidable because the sailor who wrote the poem did not witness all the proceedings or have access to Billy's thoughts.

Given the dubious nature of the foretopman's account, however, even Melville and his narrator must be questioned. Throughout the work, the narrator's confusing and melodramatic rendering of the story skirts between an omniscient narrative and a self-avowed secondhand tale of its own. Here, in concluding his work with the foretopman's ambiguous ballad, Melville's narrator draws attention to the ambiguity of his own account. In this sense, the "oozy weeds" seem to twist not only about Billy, but also about Melville himself, and about his authorial intent too. Melville renders his message dark, impenetrable, and unsatisfactory to the rational mind. In Melville's and the foretopman's words, Billy lies not resurrected in heaven, but at the bottom of the ocean, reconnected with his primitive, innocent, non-Christian nature.

IMPORTANT QUOTATIONS EXPLAINED

1. Habitually living with the elements and knowing little more of the land than as a beach, or rather, that portion . . . set apart for dance-houses, doxies, and tapsters, in short what sailors call a "fiddler's green," his simple nature remained unsophisticated by those moral obliquities which are not in every case incompatible with that manufacturable thing known as respectability. But are sailors, frequenters of fiddlers' greens, without vices? No; but less often than with landsmen do their vices, so called, partake of crookedness of heart, seeming less to proceed from viciousness than exuberance of vitality after long constraint; frank manifestations in accordance with natural law. By his original constitution aided by the co-operating influences of his lot, Billy in many respects was little more than a sort of upright barbarian, much such perhaps as Adam presumably might have been ere the urbane Serpent wriggled himself into his company.

In this quotation from Chapter 2, the narrator suggests that sailors are less likely to be wicked than men on land, since they are not exposed to difficult moral situations. Although sailors may drink and consort with prostitutes when on shore, thus gaining a sullied reputation, supposedly respectable people actually encounter more serious moral problems. Unlike people who spend most of their time on land, sailors do not commit vice out of "crookedness of heart" or "viciousness"—in other words, evil. Rather, they act sinfully because they have been confined at sea for a long time and have "natural" inclinations and an abundance of energy. Thus, although Billy has spent most of his time either on a ship or in areas of towns devoted to vice, he has nevertheless preserved his near-total ignorance of evil. Billy, if not the full-fledged physical and moral Handsome Sailor ideal, is so innocent that he stands out as an "upright barbarian" nonetheless. The last line subtly foreshadows the arrival of Claggart, who does tempt Billy to evil like the serpent. Significantly, the narrator describes the serpent as "urbane"—urbanity signifying sophistication and being the opposite of innocence. Thus, Melville equates evil with experience in society.

2.   "And now, Dansker, do tell me what you think of
     it." The old man, shoving up the front of his tarpaulin
     and deliberately rubbing the long slant scar at the
     point where it entered the thin hair, laconically said,
     "Baby Budd, *Jemmy Legs* is down on you." "*Jemmy
     Legs!*" ejaculated Billy, his welkin eyes expanding.
     "What for? Why, he calls me 'the sweet and pleasant
     young fellow,' they tell me." "Does he so?" grinned
     the grizzled one; then said, "Ay, Baby lad, a sweet
     voice has Jemmy Legs." "No, not always. But to me he
     has. I seldom pass him but there comes a pleasant
     word." "And that's because he's down upon you,
     Baby Budd."

This passage occurs in Chapter 9, when Billy, baffled about why he
seems to be having so many problems on the ship, asks the Dansker
for advice, and receives the old sailor's warning that Claggart
(called "Jemmy Legs" by the men) is his enemy. The quote is important because it represents Billy's first hint that there could be a discrepancy between someone's actions and intentions—in other
words, that Claggart could treat him with "a sweet voice" and still
hate him. Billy's baffled reaction to the Dansker's world-weary
advice shows the depth of his innocence: whereas most people mistrust each other simply out of habit, it seems almost impossible for
Billy not to trust Claggart. Billy also shows that even though he has
the ability to perceive evil, he cannot conceive of the possibility that
someone could treat him kindly and wish him harm at the same
time. In fact, the narrator goes on to note that Billy becomes almost
as troubled by the Dansker's replies as he is by the unexplained mystery of his trouble on the ship, indicating further that Billy cannot
delve beneath the surface to interpret meaning.

QUOTATIONS

3.   For what can more partake of the mysterious than
     an antipathy spontaneous and profound such as is
     evoked in certain exceptional mortals by the mere
     aspect of some other mortal, however harmless he
     may be, if not called forth by this very
     harmlessness itself?

This somewhat convoluted question from Chapter 11 represents
Melville's diagnosis of Claggart's evil, similar to his earlier description of the nature of Billy's innocence. Melville essentially argues
that Claggart's hatred of Billy stems from Billy's very "harmlessness." In other words, Claggart's "spontaneous and profound"
hatred rises due to Billy's "mere aspect"—something in Billy's
nature, or his innocent face, but nothing to do with any ill will on
Billy's part. The nature of evil is to destroy innocence, and, dimly
perceiving Billy to be somehow above the world of subterfuge and
cruelty that he himself inhabits, Claggart becomes consumed with
the desire to corrupt and destroy Billy.

QUOTATIONS

4. With no power to annul the elemental evil in him,
    though readily enough he could hide it; apprehending
    the good, but powerless to be it; a nature like
    Claggart's, surcharged with energy as such natures
    almost invariably are, what recourse is left to it but to
    recoil upon itself and, like the scorpion for which the
    Creator alone is responsible, act out to the end the
    part allotted it.

This quote, from Chapter 12, further describes the nature of Claggart's evil. Here, Melville focuses on the innate quality of Claggart's evil, a quality unusual among literary portrayals of villains. Most villains appear evil either because of events that have corrupted them or because of deliberate, avoidable choices they have made—evil resulting from a painful background or from a conscious decision to betray good. Claggart's evil has no such antecedent. Claggart simply embodies evil. Melville makes this fact clear in this description when he writes that Claggart can understand goodness, but is "powerless" to embrace it, just as he has no power to overcome the "elemental evil" that lies inside of him. Claggart has one option in life: to "act out to the end" the part that he has been assigned, that of the devious villain. Yet, if Claggart is a prisoner of his own evil, and has no choice but to act according to his evil nature, then the question arises as to whether he bears responsibility for his actions.

5.   "Struck dead by an angel of God! Yet the angel
      must hang!"

Vere speaks these words in Chapter 20, as he commits himself to
pursuing the letter of the law and seeking the death penalty for Billy
despite his own feelings. Vere equates Billy with an "angel of God,"
but at the same time says that even if a *real* angel of God had committed murder on his ship, the angel would have to hang. Vere's
duty is to oversee the application of the written law, and the law pre-
scribes hanging as a punishment for murder, particularly when the
murderous act could be attributed to a conspiratorial plot of
mutiny. In choosing to obey law over conscience, Vere commits
himself to society at the expense of own individuality. Before he
dies, he appears to rue this decision—his last words, "Billy Budd,"
apparently indicate that he dies haunted by his perceived betrayal of
the young sailor whom he admired. Reminiscent of Kant's famous
claim that justice must happen though the heavens fall, the quote
simultaneously connects Billy's plight to the religious allegory of the
novel and the question of justice. In this quote, Billy almost recalls
the devil himself. The Bible asserts that Lucifer originated as an
angel in heaven who fell from grace.

KEY FACTS

FULL TITLE

Given in various editions as *Billy Budd*; *Billy Budd, Foretopman*; and *Billy Budd, Sailor (An Inside Narrative)*. The last seems to represent Melville's final intention before he died.

AUTHOR

Herman Melville

TYPE OF WORK

Novel

GENRE

Sea story, Christian allegory, novella, philosophical novel

LANGUAGE

English

TIME AND PLACE WRITTEN

1886–1891, New York City

DATE OF FIRST PUBLICATION

1924

PUBLISHER

Constable & Company, Ltd.

NARRATOR

The story is narrated in an omniscient third person voice whose liveliness, strong opinions, and stylistic inconsistency give the narrator a forceful, erratic personality that colors the events of the story. The narrator jumps freely from character to character in describing backgrounds, attitudes, and mindsets, yet often admits ignorance concerning certain events.

POINT OF VIEW

The narrator generally focuses on Billy's point of view, but in certain chapters shifts to that of Claggart and Vere. For brief moments, the point of view of minor characters such as Captain Graveling is represented.

TONE

The narrator's attitude toward his story is generally one of ironic disillusionment. The notes of hope, reconciliation, and optimism that creep into the text, especially toward the end, have been interpreted by some readers as sincere and by others as satirical.

TENSE

Past

SETTING (TIME)

Summer of 1797, four years into the Napoleonic Wars between England and France and several months after the Great Mutiny at Nore

SETTING (PLACE)

On an English warship, the *Bellipotent,* somewhere on the Mediterranean Sea

PROTAGONIST

Billy Budd

MAJOR CONFLICT

On one level, the conflict of the book is between the natural innocence and goodness of Billy and the subtlety and deceptiveness of evil, represented by Claggart. The second major conflict of the book is the dilemma about whether Vere should absolve Billy for killing Claggart, since Billy is fundamentally innocent, or whether he should execute him to avoid appearing lenient toward mutiny.

RISING ACTION

Billy's persecution for minor infractions, his spilling the soup in front of Claggart, and his encounter with the afterguardsman, who may have been seeking to entrap him, all bring Billy and Claggart toward open conflict.

CLIMAX

Billy strikes Claggart dead after being falsely accused of mutiny.

FALLING ACTION

Vere forms a special drumhead court to try Billy, and pressures the court to convict and condemn him; Billy is executed in front of the entire crew; Billy's legend gradually begins to spread among the sailors.

THEMES

The individual versus society; conscience versus law; the vulnerability of innocence

MOTIFS

Christian allegory; suggestive names; mutiny

SYMBOLS

The ships, the purser, the surgeon

FORESHADOWING

The Dansker's warning that Claggart hates Billy; the intimations of mutiny made to Billy in the darkness

KEY FACTS

Study Questions & Essay Topics

Study Questions

1. *Does Billy Budd face his trial at the hands of a kangaroo court, one that is characterized by irresponsible, unauthorized, or irregular status or procedures? If Billy's trial is illegitimate, how does its illegitimacy relate to the overall theme of the novel?*

Some members of the ship's crew question Captain Vere's right to pass such swift judgment upon Billy, and, to a certain extent, their misgivings are reasonable. The assembled jury is certainly competent enough, yet Vere takes the dubious dual role as chief witness *and* direct superior, or judge. Melville shows that illegitimate courts prevail in a time of war. Moreover, because Melville insists that life fundamentally exists in a state of perpetual war and natural depravity; to him, life is nothing more than a kangaroo court. Indeed, the narrator points out that when the crew members begin to "murmur" following the trial and Billy's execution, the superiors on the ship quickly squelch these grumblings by blowing their whistles, forcing the men back to their duties.

2.   *What moral issues arise with the jury's decision to
sentence Billy to death? Do you think the jury makes the
right decision?*

Here we have the classic dilemma between the spirit and the letter of
the law, or, as Vere frames it, the conflict between conscience and
law. Because laws exist to support the integrity of a society and
because laws receive their strength from those who enforce them,
logic calls for the equal and firm application of those laws. Traditionally, people think of justice as being blind, and for good reason:
once the adjudicator begins to base his judgments on mitigating,
particular, or personal circumstances and considerations, he threatens the very fabric of the law and, by extension, the very fabric of
society. However, the firm application of the law means little if that
law itself is unjust. Despite the logic of Captain Vere's arguments,
especially as applied during a time of war, we are likely to be left
feeling that Billy is sacrificed unnecessarily to the greater glory of an
abstract, dehumanized cause. In most courts of law, intention and
motivation carries weight in the consideration of an action. What
might be considered wrongdoing when performed in the service of a
noble cause, is undoubtedly justified. This constant sensitivity eventually inspires the revision and improvement of laws, representing
how the just prevail in their revolution against the iniquitous hand
of their oppressors.

In Billy's case, the jury initially questions, but ultimately con-
forms to Vere's harsh reliance upon military justice, a system of law
that rejects consideration of motive and intention. Certainly, the
question of whether Billy is truly guilty of treason due to his silence
concerning a possible conspiracy complicates matters. Yet, judging
based upon what they know, the jury still makes the unjust decision
to condemn a man without considering his situation.

3.   *Ultimately, who bears the most responsibility for Billy's death: Claggart, Vere, or Billy himself?*

This is one of the many difficult problems that Melville's book raises. A strong argument could be made against the provocative Claggart, who drove Billy to the deed in an act of bald contempt. One could say that Claggart got what he deserved for he knowingly dragging Billy down with him in the process of his muckraking.

On the other hand, it was Billy himself who made the largest transgression, committing homicide in the face of a simple, if mean-spirited, accusation. All he had to do was simply defend a verbal accusation with a verbal defense, and the Captain, doubtful as he was of Claggart's allegation, probably would have dismissed the matter entirely.

Finally, one could pin the ultimate blame on Captain Vere, the inflexible stickler who insists on carrying out the law to the exact letter, even against his own better judgment. In placing principles above people, one could argue that Vere has committed the gravest sin of all, moreover attempting to wash his hands of responsibility in the very process.

Still, Melville shows that Vere operates under the negative influence of greater forces, social situations, and laws motivated by a hunger for power and a drive to war. In this sense, Melville draws attention to the idea that, in the modern world, people grow up in an inherently flawed and evil society that causes them to harden to the needs of their fellow human beings. Therefore, this laundry list of guilty parties could go on and on, including men like the Dansker as well.

SUGGESTED ESSAY TOPICS

1. How does war function in *Billy Budd*, both in the narrative itself and in the allegory? Which images symbolize war? How does war affect law? Thinking about the romantic tales of Captain Graveling and the narrator's descriptions of Captain Nelson, how does the war of the past differ from the warfare at the time the novel takes place? According to Melville, what ultimately accounts for this difference?

2. What role does the chaplain play on the ship? How is he perceived by the crewmen and Billy, respectively? What impact does he have on the novel's exploration of religious and moral themes?

3. Why might Melville have called *Billy Budd* "an inside narrative"? What do you make of the controversy over the novel's title? Does the title of the book have any bearing on how we interpret the story?

4. What role does irony play in *Billy Budd*? To what extent is the novel sincere?

5. In what ways does Melville dramatize the conflict between a person's inner self and that person's role in society? In particular, think about the Dansker, Captain Vere, and the jury.

QUESTIONS & ESSAYS

REVIEW & RESOURCES

QUIZ

1. When did Herman Melville complete *Billy Budd*?

   A. One year after the events of the novel occur, in 1798
   B. At the height of his career, in 1876
   C. The manuscript was left unfinished at his death in 1891
   D. Just in time for its first publication, in 1924

2. What is Billy Budd's nickname on the *Bellipotent*?

   A. Billy-Boy
   B. Bubbles
   C. Baby
   D. Buddy

3. What is Billy's nationality?

   A. American
   B. English
   C. Irish
   D. Kiwi

4. Why is Billy's past mysterious?

   A. He was left in a basket on a doorstep as an infant
   B. He was separated at birth from his identical twin
   C. He spontaneously generated a third eye at the age of six
   D. He ran away from home as a young boy

5. What is Billy Budd's disability?

   A. Attention Deficit Disorder
   B. Hemophilia
   C. Stuttering
   D. Dysentery

6.   To what stereotype does Billy conform?

    A.   Handsome Sailor
    B.   Mama's Boy
    C.   Hunk of Burning Love
    D.   Renaissance Man

7.   On which ship does Billy work at the opening of the novel?

    A.   The *Bellipotent*
    B.   The *Indomitable*
    C.   The *Rights-of-Man*
    D.   The *Declaration-of-Independence*

8.   What is Billy's position on the H.M.S. *Bellipotent*?

    A.   First Mate
    B.   Key Grip
    C.   Coxswain
    D.   Foretopman

9.   What is the name of the old sailor whom Billy consults from time to time?

    A.   The Danzig
    B.   The Danskin
    C.   The Dansker
    D.   The Dunster

10.   What is Claggart's position on the *Bellipotent*?

    A.   Fo'c'sleman
    B.   Lieutenant
    C.   Man-E-Faces
    D.   Master-at-arms

11.   By what nickname do the crew of the *Bellipotent* refer to Claggart?

    A.   Chukka Chukka
    B.   Jemmy Legs
    C.   Spermaceti
    D.   Bunco Boy

12. What does Billy spill in front of Claggart?

    A.   His soup
    B.   Some milk
    C.   The beans
    D.   A pan of oatmeal

13. For what does the mysterious afterguardsman try to recruit Billy?

    A.   A refrigerator raid
    B.   A midnight game of dice
    C.   A conspiracy to commit mutiny
    D.   A drug ring

14. What crime does Claggart accuse Billy of committing?

    A.   Perjury
    B.   Dereliction
    C.   Desertion
    D.   Conspiracy

15. How does Billy respond to Claggart's accusation?

    A.   By punching Claggart in the head
    B.   By denying everything
    C.   By committing suicide
    D.   By stabbing Claggart in the heart

16. What does Claggart do a few moments after accusing Billy to his face?

    A.   Takes back his accusation
    B.   Abandons ship
    C.   Challenges Billy to a duel
    D.   Lies dead on the cabin floor

17. What is Captain Vere's nickname?

    A.   The Nutty Professor
    B.   Perse Vere
    C.   Starry Vere
    D.   The Chronic

18. How does Captain Vere decide to respond to the killing of Claggart?

    A. By calling a drumhead court
    B. By covering up the whole affair in an effort to save Billy Budd
    C. By "fiddling while Rome burns"
    D. By suspending judgment until they reach home shores

19. What is Billy Budd formally accused of before the court?

    A. Larceny
    B. Assault
    C. Conspiracy
    D. Homicide

20. What is the court's sentence on Billy Budd?

    A. An afternoon in the pillory
    B. Community service
    C. Ten years of hard labor
    D. Death by hanging

21. What is Billy's reaction to his sentence?

    A. A violent outburst against his judges
    B. Passive acceptance of his fate
    C. An eloquent defense of his innocence
    D. He busts out crying, like the little baby that he is

22. Who visits Billy on the eve of his execution?

    A. Captain Vere
    B. The Dansker
    C. The ship's chaplain
    D. Ishmael

23. When is Billy Budd hung?

    A. Dawn
    B. High noon
    C. Dusk
    D. Midnight

24. What are Billy Budd's last words?

   A. God bless America!
   B. God save the Queen!
   C. God bless Captain Vere!
   D. My God, my God, why have you forsaken me?

25. Who writes the poem "Billy in the Darbies"?

   A. Billy Budd
   B. The Dansker
   C. Captain Vere
   D. Some other sailor

SUGGESTIONS FOR FURTHER READING

HARDWICK, ELIZABETH. *Herman Melville.* New York: Penguin, 2000.

HOWARD, LEON. *Herman Melville.* Minneapolis: University of Minnesota Press, 1961.

LEVINE, ROBERT, ed. *The Cambridge Companion to Herman Melville.* New York: Cambridge University Press, 1998.

MUMFORD, LEWIS. *Herman Melville: A Study of His Life and Vision.* New York: Harcourt, Brace, 1962.

PARKER, HERSHEL. *Reading Billy Budd.* Evanston, Illinois: Northwestern University Press, 1990.

WOOD, JAMES. "The All and the If: God and Metaphor in Melville." In *The Broken Estate: Essays on Literature and Belief.* New York: Random House, 1999.

SparkNotes
Test Preparation
Guides

The SparkNotes team figured it was time to cut standardized tests down to size. We've studied the tests for you, so that SparkNotes test prep guides are:

Smarter:
Packed with critical-thinking skills and test-
taking strategies that will improve your score.

Better:
Fully up to date, covering all new features of the tests,
with study tips on every type of question.

Faster:
Our books cover exactly what you need to
know for the test. No more, no less.

SparkNotes Guide to the SAT & PSAT
SparkNotes Guide to the SAT & PSAT — Deluxe Internet Edition
SparkNotes Guide to the ACT
SparkNotes Guide to the ACT — Deluxe Internet Edition
SparkNotes Guide to the SAT II Writing
SparkNotes Guide to the SAT II U.S. History
SparkNotes Guide to the SAT II Math Ic
SparkNotes Guide to the SAT II Math IIc
SparkNotes Guide to the SAT II Biology
SparkNotes Guide to the SAT II Physics

SparkNotes Study Guides: